Slavenka Drakulić, born in Croatia in 1949, is a writer and journalist whose two novels (*Holograms of Fear* and *Marble Skin*) and three non-fiction books (*How We Survived Communism and Even Laughed*, *Balkan Express* and *Café Europa*) have been translated into major European languages. Her new novel *The Taste of a Man* will be published by Abacus in 1997. She contributes to *The New Republic*, *La Stampa*, *Dagens Nyheter*, *Frankfurter Rundschau*, *The Observer* and her writing has appeared in magazines and newspapers around the world. She writes both in Croatian and English.

Café
Europa

Life after Communism

SLAVENKA DRAKULIĆ

W. W. NORTON & COMPANY
New York   *London*

Library of Congress Cataloging-in-Publication Data

Drakulić, Slavenka, 1949-
    Café Europa : life after communism / Slavenka Drakulić.
       p.   cm.
    "First published in Great Britain by Abacus 1996."
    ISBN 0-393-04012-7
    1. Post-communism—Europe, Eastern. 2. Europe, Eastern—Social
conditions—1989-   3. Europe, Eastern—Politics and
government—1989-   I.   Title.
HN380.7.A8D73   1997
   306'.0947—dc20   96-46010 CIP

W.W. Norton & Company, Inc., 500 Fifth Avenue, New York, NY 10110
http://www.wwnorton.com
W.W. Norton & Company Ltd., 10 Coptic Street, London WC1A 1PU

1 2 3 4 5 6 7 8 9 0

For Richard, who knows it all

Contents

Introduction: First-Person Singular

The pieces in this book were written between 1992 and 1996. As I reread them, I noticed that, to my surprise, I constantly use the pronouns 'we' and 'us'. When I am speaking in my everyday life I rarely do so – quite the contrary. I can see that they come to me naturally in the context of this book, but they trouble me nonetheless.

Why do they come naturally? Am I representing some-one – a group, a party, a state? No, I am not. Am I appointed by someone? Not that I know of. Am I aware that other people think like me, and subconsciously identifying with them, even though I don't know them? No. So where do these pronouns come from, and whom do they represent? Clearly, in the context of this book, 'we' and 'us' mean the people of ex-communist countries, and as I am one of them I believe that I can justify using the first-person plural to describe our common experience. Yet, at the same time, I am annoyed by this first-person plural; I feel uneasy using it, as if I had something personal against it.

And I do. I hate the first-person plural. But it is only now, seeing it in my own writing, that I realise how much I hate it. My resistance to it is almost physical, because more than anything else, to me it represents a physical experience. I can smell the scent of bodies pressed against e in a 1 May parade, or at the celebration of Tito's birth. ay on 25 May, the sweaty armpits of a man in front of me, my own perspiration; I can feel the crowd pushing me forward, all of us moving as one, a single body – a sort of automatic puppet-like motion because no one is capable of anything else. I can feel the nausea; there is no air to breathe and I want to get out of the crowd, but my movements are restricted to a step forward or backwards in a strange ballet choreographed from a podium up above. Exhausted, I can't do anything but allow myself to be carried along until it is all over.

I grew up with 'we' and 'us': in the kindergarten, at school, in the pioneer and youth organisations, in the community, at work. I grew up listening to the speeches of politicians saying, 'Comrades, we must . . .' and with these comrades, we did what we were told, because we did not exist in any other grammatical form. Later on, I experienced the same phenomenon in journalism. It was the journalism of endless editorials, in which 'we' explained to 'us' what 'we' all needed to understand. More neutral forms of language, not as direct as 'we', were used later on, but still in the plural. It was hard to escape that plural, as if it were an iron mould, a shirt, a suit – a uniform. First-person eye-witness reports were not a popular genre of journalism precisely for this reason. In such pieces, the reporter can't claim that 'we saw it', only that 'I saw it'. He can avoid referring to himself altogether, but he is still by definition present in his story. Writing meant testing out the borders of both language and genres, pushing them away from editorials and first-person plural and towards the first-person singular. The consequences of using the first-person singular were often unpleasant. You stuck out; you risked being labelled an 'anarchic element' (not even a person), perhaps even a dissident. For that you would be sacked, so you used it sparingly, and at your own risk. This was called self-censorship.

That hideous first-person plural troubles me for another reason, too. I saw at first hand how dangerous it can be, how easily it can become infected by the deadly diseases of nationalism and war. The war in the Balkans is the product of that 'us', of that huge, 20 million-bodied mass swinging back and forth in waves, then following their leaders into mass hysteria. Individuals who were against that war, who saw it coming, where could they turn? To what organisation or institution? There was no organised political alternative. The individual citizen had no chance to voice his protest or his opinion, not even his fear. He could only leave the country – and so people did. Those who used 'I' instead of 'we' in their language had to escape. It was this fatal difference in grammar that divided them from the rest of their compatriots. As a consequence of this 'us', no civic society developed. The little there was, in the form of small, isolated and marginalised groups, was soon swallowed up by the national homogenisation that did not permit any differences, any individualism. As under communism, individualism was punished – individuals speaking out against the war, or against nationalism, were singled out as 'traitors'.

How does a person who is a product of a totalitarian society learn responsibility, individuality, initiative? By saying 'no'. But this begins with saying 'I', thinking 'I' and doing 'I' – and in public as well as in private. Individuality, the first-person singular, always existed under communism, it was just exiled from public and political life and exercised in private. Thus the terrible hypocrisy with which we learned to live in order to survive is having its backlash now: it is very difficult to connect the private and public 'I'; to start believing that an individual opinion, initiative or vote really could make a difference. There is still too big a danger that the citizen will withdraw into an anonymous, safe 'us'. But now attitudes differ from country to country. With the collapse of communism, the individual countries started to emancipate themselves from their collective status and to distinguish themselves from their neighbours.

So in Eastern European countries, the difference between 'we' and 'I' is to me far more important than mere grammar. 'We' means fear, resignation, submissiveness, a warm crowd and somebody else deciding your destiny. 'I' means giving individuality and democracy a chance.

Individualism is flourishing in one respect in Eastern Europe. It is visible only in the ruthless accumulation of capital. Perhaps a chance to make money, a chance those people never had before, is indeed a condition to developing the first-person singular. Why, then, have I used 'we' and 'us' so frequently in this book? Because a common denominator is still discernible, and still connects us all, often against our will. It is not only our communist past, but also the way we would like to escape from it, the direction in which we want to go. It's our longing for Europe and all that it stands for. Or, rather, what we imagine Europe stands for. I believe you can see this common denominator if you take a close look at the price of bananas, at our bad teeth and public toilets, or at our yards on the outskirts of big cities. Indeed, you can see it merely by taking a walk on any boulevard in any capital, be it Tirana or Budapest, Prague or Warsaw. Somewhere there will be a hotel, a cinema, a bar, a restaurant, a café or a simple hole in the wall, named, for our desire, Europa.

Café Europa

Vienna seems to be very popular in Sofia, judging by the *konditoreien*, or coffee shops – there are at least two named after it. Through the window of one of them, on the Boulevard of the Tzar Liberator, people can be seen sitting at small, round cast-iron tables painted white. The coffee served there is not the traditional kind, called 'Bulgarian coffee' (or Macedonian, Turkish, Serbian or Greek coffee, depending on where it is drunk), roughly ground and cooked in small brass pots. Here the coffee is prepared differently and served in big cups with whipped cream and cinnamon or chocolate on top, just like in Vienna. There are also several kinds of 'Viennese' cakes and tarts sitting in a glass cupboard lit by a neon strip, which turns a yellow vanilla cream cake into a greenish one and gives a sickly grey hue to the peaches and strawberries on the tarts. They are nothing like real Viennese cakes, elaborate, rich and opulent; in fact, there is nothing in this café reminiscent of the big European city, except its name.

The other 'Viennese' coffee shop looks a bit better. It is

small and the walls are painted in pastel pink and café-au-lait. Youngsters are seated at round, fake-marble tables, most of them drinking tea, probably because that is all they can afford here – the prices tend to be Viennese, too. But the nice thing about this café is that with your tea you get a small biscuit on a paper doily, just as, I suppose, it is served in Vienna. This kind of sophistication is very new in this part of the world.

Yet when I am in Vienna, or any other Western capital, I am not usually conscious of how tea or coffee is served, perhaps because I take it for granted that it will be presented in a certain way and therefore I don't pay any attention to it. For me it would be a surprise only if it were served in some other, strange – say, Eastern European way – a single kind of black tea only, or several cups produced from a single teabag, with no milk let alone lemon, spilling over into the saucer. And, most likely, the teacup would be white with a blue rim, like the ones you get at school or in a factory canteen. In Sofia, however, elegant presentation has a Brechtian alienation effect. Because it is not expected, one notices it immediately. Indeed, the whole of the Café Wien projects a certain image of Western Europe – pastel-coloured, over-decorated, clean, cute, orderly, even if that image does not necessarily have anything to do with reality.

Tirana is no exception to this trend of giving foreign names to just about any place. Café Europa, and there seems to be more than one, is situated in the centre of the city. It is a kind of kiosk, one of 2,000 similar constructions of glass and metal that grew up there in just two years. On a sunny day you can see a lot of people sitting outside it in white plastic seats, drinking an excellent espresso. I can only suppose that these plastic seats, which would in the

West be thought in bad taste, are considered both elegant and exotic in Albania, since such furniture was neither produced nor even seen in the country until recently. The customers are mostly young men, smoking heavily and listening to boomingly loud rock or disco music. Imagine a friend asking you where you are going, and you say, 'I'm going to the Europa.' Sounds good, doesn't it? To sit like that, dressed in a faded pair of jeans, and wearing your hair long, must be one of the most important and most visible elements of new freedom to them.

Bucharest does not lag behind Tirana or Sofia. It has a lot of small private shops, not very beautiful or expensive, but whose names clearly suggest Westernisation. Even if it is only a hole in the wall, it will have a name like Point West. Any food shop will be a supermarket, regardless of the fact that as it stocks only about twenty products, it can hardly be considered a market, much less a supermarket. And nearby, if you want, you can enjoy your coffee in a café with another very evocative Western name: Hollywood.

If you find yourself on any of the main boulevards of Budapest, you will inevitably notice that almost all the shops are owned by large foreign companies – McDonald's, Coca-Cola, Shell, Benetton, to name just a few of the better-known ones. It is hard to find any Hungarian-sounding name among them. You have the feeling that you must be in Vienna or Paris – except that the buildings are a bit too shabby, people are dressed differently, the streetcars are a little too crowded, and there are still many old Trabant and Lada cars driving around. But I am sure that in no Western European capital can you buy sweets in a shop with a name like Bonbonnière Hemingway. The owner must be an admirer of the writer; or perhaps he is not aware that it is a writer's name, but just likes the sound of it.

In Prague, Zagreb, Bratislava or Ljubljana and other Eastern European cities, towns – even villages – you can eat, drink, sleep, dress or entertain yourself in places with Western European and, to a lesser extent, American names. Bonjour, Target, Four Roses, Lady, The End. This is such a widespread phenomenon that in extremely nationalist countries, such as Croatia, voices are already being raised in protest. A journalist on the main daily newspaper there expressed his serious concern, reasoning that tourists visiting Zagreb might be confused, and think that they were in England instead! This would be laughable if it was not the subject of serious discussion in the Croatian parliament, where a representative has proposed a law that would oblige all firms to use Croatian names.

But what that journalist did not understand, of course, is that this is precisely the point of Western names: to create the impression that you are already in the West. No nationalistic ideology could stamp out the desire to prove that Zagreb and Croatia belong to the West, not even the introduction of such an absurd law. On the surface, this practice seems merely a trick to attract customers. But it has a deeper significance in that it symbolises how people in these countries see themselves – or rather, where they would like to see themselves. Nowadays, across Eastern Europe, revolution no longer consists of introducing democracy and a free-market economy; this has already happened. It might not work as was expected, but it is there nonetheless. Instead revolution is seen in small, everyday things: sounds, looks and images.

Foreign names are an excellent shorthand for conveying the message of this revolution. Simply by using such a name, you are presenting not only an image, but a whole system of values, too. They also reveal a longing, a desire to belong to a preconceived idea of Western Europe. At the same time they serve as a kind of a barrier, because they seek to deny the old communist Eastern Europe. In fact, there can never be enough signs to indicate and emphasise that indeed this is not the old, communist, poor, primitive, Oriental, backward Eastern Europe any longer. Can't you see that we belong to the West too, except that we have been exiled from it for half a century?

If you asked a child riding a broomstick what it was doing, the child would answer, without hesitation: 'I am riding a horse.' For that child, a stick *is* a horse. It is as if by merely calling something by another name, you are able to transform it into what you want it to be. By usurping God's power, you create an illusion of an instant Paradise. And no one has yet told the infant Eastern Europe that a wooden stick is not a horse.

Imagine the opposite situation, a sudden flood in Paris or in London, of names like Tirana, Durres, Belgrade, Orient, or even *Napredak* (progress) or *Pobjeda* (victory) – typical communist names. It is not that such establishments don't exist in Europe's capitals, but the very few that do are sad meeting places for nostalgic emigrants. They in no way represent a desire to be different, to be a part of Eastern Europe. In Vienna, one Café Europa, in the Karntner-strasse, the city's main pedestrian zone, is a part of The Hotel Europa. The other Café Europa is an obscure bar near Mariahilferstrasse, dark, noisy, stinking of beer. There is also a third one near the Belvedere Palace. None of them represents any kind of culture, because there is no need for a special kind of representation. There are no extraordinary cultural values attached to either the name or their decor.

In 1990 – when Croatia, as a newly independent state, wanted to distance itself as far as possible from the other, non-European part of former Yugoslavia, from the Serbian enemy – the most beautiful cinema in Zagreb was renamed the Europa. Its previous name, for many decades, had been the Balkan. All of a sudden, the old name was seen as a symbol of the past, of primitivism, of the war, of something 'non-European'. The new name is heavily loaded with a complexity of positive values. In the first place, it is a symbol of a more distant past. It indicates that Croatia was part of the Austro–Hungarian empire until the end of the First World War, while Serbia, situated deep in the Balkans (Croats don't view their country as being part of the Balkans), was under Turkish rule for 500 years. It is also intended to suggest that Croatia always belonged to the more developed part of Europe, and to the Catholic religion, as opposed to the Orthodox religion of their neighbours. It represents Christian tolerance, civilised behaviour and bourgeois values. 'Europa' encapsulates what the people aspire to, not what they really are – as if by changing the name of a cinema we can at a stroke remove ourselves from the Balkans and enter 'Europa' whatever that means.

In using such a name as Europa, there is an assumption that everyone knows what we mean by Europe. One thing is sure: it is no longer the name of an entire continent. It describes only one part of it, the western part, in a geographical, cultural, historical and political sense. Europe has been divided by the different historical development of its component parts, communism and most of all by poverty. Some formerly western countries, like Czechoslovakia and Hungary, found themselves in the Eastern bloc. Now it looks as if all of the ex-communist, Eastern European countries have the same almost palpable wish to push that dividing line as far to the east as possible, so that eventually Europe will be a whole, undivided continent. Yet it is this desire itself which forms the current dividing line. The West does not feel the need to belong (it just *is*) or to allow the countries standing at its threshold to enter. It waits to pick the lucky ones who will meet its standards and join the European Council, NATO or some other of its institutions.

So, what does Europe mean in the Eastern European imagination? It is certainly not a question of geography, for in those terms we are already in it and need make no effort to reach it. It is something distant, something to be attained, to be deserved. It is also something expensive and fine: good clothes, the certain look and smell of its people. Europe is plenitude: food, cars, light, everything – a kind of festival of colours, diversity, opulence, beauty. It offers choice: from shampoo to political parties. It represents freedom of expression. It is a promised land, a new Utopia, a lollipop. And through television, that Europe is right there, in your apartment, often in colours much too bright to be real.

Yet all this doesn't get us very far in terms of definition; it simply explains the desire itself. The negative approach is perhaps more useful: Europe is the opposite of what we have, and what we want to get rid of – it is the absence of communism, of fear and deprivation. The Bosnian writer Djevad Karahasan describes Hotel Europa, an old Austro–Hungarian establishment in the middle of Sarajevo, as a geographical and cultural point where West and East met. The hotel was destroyed in the shelling; Europe thus disappeared from Sarajevo. It left Sarajevo because most of the country, the city, and its people left, too, deceived by Europe. So Europe has many faces, and we should not forget that.

Is anyone today able to say where Europe, and all it stands for, begins, and where it ends? Does the new political reality call for a broader definition? Perhaps the idea that an Eastern European country has to deserve Europe, that it has to qualify for it in some way, is now becoming too conservative. After all, in the United States a hundred years ago, black people were *a priori* excluded from the definition of that continent. Today, the Afro–American population and its contribution to the United States cannot be separated from America itself. Perhaps there is something positive and valuable that the Eastern European nations have to contribute to the Europe of today. Is it arts, multi-culturalism, diversity in general? Is it the model of the moral politician, represented by Vaclav Havel? Or is it the most important human skill of all: the ability to just survive in impossible conditions?

Europe is not a mother who owes something to her long-neglected children; neither is she a princess one has to court. She is not a knight sent to free us, nor an apple or a cake to be enjoyed; she is not a silk dress, nor the magic word 'democracy'. Most likely, Europe is what we – countries, peoples, individuals – make of it for ourselves.

Invisible Walls Between Us

I looked into my passport and panicked. My American visa had just expired. Funnily enough, it was not because I was about to visit the United States that I panicked: it is a habit I have as a citizen of a former communist country. I simply know that when I have a one-year multiple-entry American visa, it is much easier to enter any other Western European country. My experience of many years tells me that.

But now we are in the year 1995 and I no longer live in communist Yugoslavia, but in democratic Croatia. Similar is the case of Romanians, Poles and Bulgarians, for that matter. Why, then, has my fear of borders not gone? Why do I feel as nervous going west as ever before? What has really changed for we Eastern Europeans when we cross into Western Europe in the post-communist era? We believed that after 1989 we would be welcomed to an undivided Europe, that we would somehow officially become what we always knew we were – that is, Europeans. Finally, we would join the others, the French, the Germans, or the Swiss. But we were wrong in nourishing that illusion. Today, the proof of our status in Europe is easy to find. It awaits us at every western border crossing in the stern face of a police officer looking down upon us, even if he doesn't say a word.

This look has not changed. I know it by heart. I remember it from before – police officers at border crossings have always looked at us in that way. They knew perfectly well that this look would make us nervous, because we always had to disguise the amount of money we possessed, or to lie about the dying aunt we were supposedly visiting or just about that hidden bottle of home-made plum brandy. Then there was look number two: the screening, X-ray officer's look, suspecting everyone of wanting to get illegally employed in his country, if not – God forbid! – asking for asylum. Once you have felt that look of suspicion, you don't ever forget it and you can recognise it from miles away.

Perhaps I myself have no right to complain too much about crossing borders. I first left Yugoslavia in 1957, when I was eight years old. With my grandmother I visited an aunt in Italy. I still recall that the aunt had to write a letter of guarantee: there was much talk about it in the family – would it arrive? Would it be good enough for the authorities to let us out? I was old enough to know that not many people could travel abroad at that time, and that I was privileged. So even before the journey began, I felt elevated by the mere prospect of it. I told all my friends, all my classmates and our neighbours about it. My aunt and uncle came in their car to pick us up in Ancona. I was sick all the way to Naples – I had never travelled in a car before. All I remember from that trip is that terrible nausea. Nevertheless, when we returned home a month later, I was triumphant. It was worth it; I had 'seen the world'.

From the late fifties onwards, with each year it became easier to travel and virtually everyone in Yugoslavia possessed a passport and could go to Western Europe without a visa. This gradually became a special reason for all Yugoslavs to feel superior to the rest of the communist countries, whose citizens were forced to stay at home. At that time, Yugoslavia was well off and people could afford to travel both as tourists and as what we called 'shopping tourists', to buy what we could not get in our own country. Millions of the Yugoslavs who went abroad in the seventies, eighties and nineties were not economic or political emigrants. Quite the contrary: they went abroad in order to *spend* their money. But they were never welcomed for all that; it was as if their money was not good enough, as if it had a special, Eastern European smell.

First, the Yugoslav police would automatically suspect us because there were strict rules about taking money out of the country. It was not possible to change our money into foreign currency at the bank, so we had to buy what we needed on the black market. Yet, if we then put the illegally exchanged money into the bank, and obtained a certificate for it, we could take abroad a permitted amount – say $US150, and no one would ask us where it came from. However, the bank certificate was just a piece of paper that served as a cover-up for a larger, hidden amount, and so we were in constant fear of the border police. They knew that we would have much more money with us than we were allowed to take out, and it depended on their mood whether they would start questioning us or searching us.

Then, when we entered the foreign country, their border police were not exactly delighted to see us, either. Any citizen from a communist country was by definition a suspect, so he had to be interrogated, to prove he had the money whose existence, only a while ago, he had had to deny; to confirm how long he was going to stay, where and why. In the late sixties, I remember, the best thing was to say that you were visiting a relative (you were sometimes required to produce a letter) because the border police did not believe you would have enough money to support yourself. Later on, in the seventies and eighties, it was sufficient to say that you were going shopping, even if you were not. But the general feeling of guilt would descend every time we approached a glass cabin. I always felt nervous as the policeman behind the glass looked at me, as he browsed through my passport, as if he could hardly believe that I was not a common criminal trying to escape my country.

Sometimes I took advantage of the fact that I was a woman and gave him a nice smile. It might or might not help – one never knew. Once, arriving at the airport in Paris from New York, I smiled at an officer and was immediately selected for a luggage search. Of course, I was not innocent: I had with me a laptop computer and I had to persuade the officer that I was taking it to a third country so that he would not make me pay a customs fee (one learns foreign customs rules by heart, too.) Because my next flight was not until the following morning and I had to enter France, he was entitled to make me pay it. After negotiations he let me go, but the incident only confirmed to him that we Eastern Europeans were unreliable even when we smiled, or perhaps because we did. I discovered that if you are an Eastern European there are no rules. I know people who dressed up and tried to look smart, only to be searched even more thoroughly. Perhaps well-dressed Eastern Europeans conveyed the wrong message – the impression that they were involved in illegal business, for instance. As a more casual type, I too experienced all sorts of searches – everything except the final indignity of a gynaecological examination. (Yes, I have stood naked in that little cabin that exists at every border crossing.)

Travelling abroad in those days, I had to take so many things into consideration, whereas a citizen of Western Europe did not have to pay a single thought to such concerns. This, I think, was what marked the real difference between us.

But in spite of all the difficulties, travelling was important to people from Yugoslavia, because we could do it, while the others in Eastern Europe could not. It was also a kind of rebellion against the communist state, making ourselves vulnerable to the 'contamination' of Western ideas and lifestyles. Today I see it did not work in that way. My generation in Yugoslavia was the first to travel freely, but we were already so hypocritical, and believed so little in communist ideology, that travelling abroad could not really influence us. Besides, precisely because we did travel, we knew that we were not welcome in Western Europe. But that inferiority complex was balanced by the fact that the citizens of other communist countries could not travel. It was enough to go to Prague or Budapest to feel superior. This was a big mistake, for now a cynical twist of history has turned the former Yugoslavia into the most troubled place in Europe and our apparent superiority has been destroyed.

However distrusted, discouraged or even humiliated I was when travelling, I took every chance to go abroad. I went to recharge my batteries, to buy books and see movies, to meet interesting people. Travelling for me assumed almost mythical proportions. I needed to do it because, in my mind, staying in one place all the time was almost equal to dying, and I struggled hard to scrape together the money to make it possible, at the expense of a better standard of living at home. Even today it is hard for me to decline an invitation to a conference or to lecture in a country I have not yet visited. I simply feel obliged to go; I feel I have no moral right to refuse such an offer. It is easier now, because if I am invited, usually all my expenses are paid. But it doesn't mean that anything has really changed.

My husband is Swedish. It is not important to me that he is a Westerner, except when we travel together. Recently, we were both invited to Oslo, Norway. My preparations for the trip did not run parallel with his. All my husband needed to do was to reserve a ticket and pack his suitcase at the very last moment. But I had to start much earlier, by calling the embassy in order to find out if, as a Croatian citizen, I needed a visa. In this case I did not, but when a visa is required I will need to know how long it takes to get one (a Canadian visa, for example, takes two days, because you have to travel from Zagreb to Vienna to get it), and how much it costs, as well as what documents I must present in order to get it – a student ID, a letter from my employer, a photocopy of my bank statement or written proof that I own property in my country. That is not always the end of it: some countries, like Great Britain, need further proof, that is, a letter of invitation. Someone has to act as guarantor for you – being from Eastern Europe, you are not to be trusted. Even today they are reluctant to believe that you are visiting their country on a business trip, let alone as a simple tourist. This always brings back to my memory my aunt's guarantee letter from that visit to Italy almost forty years ago.

In January I witnessed a humiliating scene at Heathrow Airport in London. An elderly Croatian couple had been interrogated because they were going on holiday to Barbados, with a stopover in London. Tourists from Croatia going to Barbados? Whoever heard of such a thing? The couple went into lengthy explanations, presenting their tickets, their hotel reservations, their visas, and perhaps their money, too, all in perfect order. In their voices I recognised the same anxiety and frustration I had often felt myself. One could tell that the young, arrogant customs officer at passport control automatically assumed that no one from that part of the world could possibly be anything other than a potential immigrant and, therefore, a danger.

My long preparations for a trip abroad are not the only difference between my Swedish husband and me. When we approach a passport-control cabin at an airport, he can just flick his passport and the official will wave his hand and let him pass without even bothering to look at it. Or, lately, he has even been able to choose the entrance for 'Domestic and EC' travellers, rather than 'Others', as I must do. The invisible wall between Easterners and Westerners starts right there, in front of a glass window with a small opening. The officer first takes my passport and inspects it carefully, as if he is not sure whether it is a forgery or not. Then he checks whether my name is on the list of dangerous criminals or other wanted people. His first question is: 'How long do you intend to stay?' It is usually enough to show him my ticket, and he does not go on asking questions. If he does, I know that he will ask me: 'How much money do you have?' This question makes my blood boil. Does the fact that you come from Western Europe automatically qualify you as a well-off person? But I am well prepared for this response, too, so I suppress my rage and show him the traveller's cheques that I carry with me solely for this purpose. If he still insists on asking me where

I am staying, I show him a letter of invitation, indicating that, after all, I am *invited* to his bloody country, not an intruder. This might – just might – gain me some respect, but even so it is a false respect: he still mistrusts me because he thinks that the letter might be a fake. By now, I feel poor, smeared and embarrassed, and that is the mood in which I take my first steps in a Western country.

Do I need to stress that my Swedish husband does not have to answer any of these questions? Simply, he never gets asked them.

Perhaps this is what Purgatory is like, I say to myself as I am about to pass to the other side. My eyes, accustomed to border-crossing scenes, glance at a small group of gipsies, Albanians or Bosnian refugees, separated even from us in order to be really humiliated. And as I look at them for a moment, I know, they know and the police officers know that barriers do exist and that citizens from Eastern Europe are going to be second-class citizens still for a long time to come, regardless of the downfall of communism or the latest political proclamations. Between us and them there is an invisible wall. Europe is a divided continent, and only those who could not travel to see it for themselves believed that Easterners and Westerners could become equal. The simple truth, which I can read in the police officer's eyes, is that we are not. Moreover, it seems to me that the citizens of the new democratic countries are suspected even more than before, since more of them are able to travel abroad than in the past.

I am worried about my marriage. If this kind of segregation goes on for too long, I will have a hard time convincing my husband that I have married him for love, and not just to have him standing behind me at some passport control at a Western European border in order to say the magic words: 'She is my wife.'

Why I Never Visited Moscow

It happened at one of the literary festivals in
England in 1995. When I first started to attend
these, at the end of the eighties, the idea of a
literary festival confused me. I was used to something pretty
different, namely literary congresses, that is to say, endless
discussions about writers and political power, about cen-
sorship, self-censorship and the importance of being a
writer in general, rather than about literature itself. Later
on, after some experience of festivals abroad, I found the
idea of celebrating literature – having readings, talking
about literature outside the obligatory political context –
rather refreshing.

At this particular festival, after my own reading, I was
invited to take part in a round-table discussion about the
situation of writers in Eastern Europe after the collapse of
communism. There were about ten of us, writers from all
over Eastern Europe. I remember Albanian, Romanian,
Czech, Polish, Russian and Hungarian writers, sitting in a
semi-circle, facing the public with a certain feeling of
anxiety. We were aware that we were scarcely able to

express ourselves properly in English and we didn't know what we were supposed to say. It was kindly suggested to each of us by the organisers that we started off by telling our personal story, and then came up with some general ideas and conclusions about how life in our countries had changed for writers, artists and intellectuals.

I felt uncomfortable with the implied division between Them and Us, the Eastern Europeans. I did not like sitting on a panel with whose members I had nothing in common, not even language, except for the fact that we all came from former communist countries in the same part of the world. Why do we still have to be thrown into the same basket, be it communism or ex-communism? I asked. When will we finally have the right to be accepted for what we are, that is individual writers with our own names and books? After all, I did not see any panel of Western European or even British writers discussing the political, social or economic issues of their own countries and feeling obliged to have an opinion on them. In spite of my belief that in the previous few years we had finally moved on from having to do this, on this occasion in Cheltenham we were once again summoned together and expected to talk about everything, from political changes to war, religion and unemployment. There was a difference now, and it was that before, it was the public in our own countries that had expected this of us, whereas now it was the foreign public, subscribing to the persistent cliché of the Eastern European writer as the conscience of his people. It seemed as if we couldn't easily escape this role, I told the audience in Cheltenham. By being asked to participate in that round-table discussion, we were obviously expected to confirm the general prejudice about the Eastern European writer, rather than to say what it was we wanted to say.

I don't know if some of my colleagues felt the same but were too polite to say what was really in their hearts. Probably they felt obliged to our kind hosts, because for most of us the only possibility of travelling to the West is by being invited to such a round-table discussion, with our tickets paid for, a room in a nice hotel and some pocket money. We might be free now, but we are still very poor. So it was not easy for my colleagues to speak up on this issue. One writer, from my country, evidently did not agree in any case, for she responded quickly with exactly the opposite view. How pathetic your attempt is to distance yourself from other writers from former communist countries, she said, when we all have the same experience that determines us, both as human beings and as writers. There is no use denying it, or trying to escape from your own past. We are stuck there together. Her tone of voice seemed to me sad, fatalistic.

There was some truth in this very deterministic view. I think that both of us were right: I, in my plea for the writer's right to individualism; she, who denied not that right, but the possibility of its realisation. And as I took a close look at the public in the room that evening, I had to admit that, yes, in the eyes of the public I must have been bracketed with the rest of that bunch of writers. The town where we attended the literary festival is a spa, and many who live there are wealthy, retired people. Since this festival was one of the very few events happening there, they came to our readings and discussions showing great interest – white-haired men with walking sticks and hearing aids, fragile, bird-like ladies with a lot of gold hanging around their necks and innocent smiles on their faces, plus a few local intellectuals, journalists and teachers of literature. Faced with their confused glances and naïve questions, I saw that there indeed was, between the writers and that public, however benevolent and sympathetic, a visible barrier. The audience simply did not have enough background information to comprehend what the writers sitting in front of them on the podium were saying. Confronted with such a lack of understanding, I felt that I had no other choice but to hang on to 'my' group, the writers from Eastern Europe. At least they knew what I was talking about; at least we understood each other's problems, if that was of any comfort to a single one of us. And in any case, even if I had loudly screamed that I didn't want to belong to any group at all, the audience would have put me with them. Perhaps for the first time I became aware of how tired I was of constantly being pushed back into 'my place' every time I made an attempt to break out.

Still I wanted to get away from our common denominator, our common past, even if, at that moment in Cheltenham, I was not quite aware of how badly I wanted it. I was soon to realise this.

Not long after the Cheltenham-episode, I found that I had accumulated enough air miles for a free flight to a city of my own choice. 'Let's go to St Petersburg,' my husband suggested enthusiastically. 'It is such a beautiful city. I am sure you would like it a lot.' Before he had a chance to continue praising St Petersburg, which he had visited several times while it was still called Leningrad, I cried out 'No!' at the top of my voice. I surprised even myself with my violent reaction to his words.

Suddenly, I had a vague feeling of panic, as if he would force me to go there, or as if some dark memory was casting its shadow over me. I am aware that such a surge of negative feelings about St Petersburg, the kind of slight nausea you get at the thought of visiting the dentist, will seem rather odd when I tell you that they were not a consequence of some bad experience I had had there. I had never been to St Petersburg; I had never even been to the former Soviet Union. So were my feelings simply the result of prejudice? And if so, could that prejudice be so strong that the idea of going there physically revolted me?

It is not easy to identify the source of my anxiety. It stems from my whole life experience in communist Yugoslavia, from my past, my education and the ideology I was surrounded by. When I think back now, I can perceive a strange absence of any impulse to visit what used to be the USSR. In my mind the USSR was some kind of huge cement block representing only one thing: a threat. This notion of mine doesn't make me much different from an average American, I suppose. While I believe that from the time of Mikhail Gorbachev's *perestroika* Americans had already started to change their attitude, I am not sure that I have changed mine at all. The difference is that I have lived under the same kind of political system, whereas they have not. I know how it works inside out; I have seen how it grinds people's lives until it turns them into dust. For me, the former Soviet Union was not much more than a giant communist grinding machine, bigger, stronger and more dangerous than the one that existed in my own country. It is hard now to revise this sort of image and erase the feeling the name St Petersburg evokes in me. I know that the only proper way to do it would be to go there, but I am avoiding that even now. This is unfair to the Russians. But nevertheless, whenever I think about going there, I feel as if I have just swallowed a snake.

If that grey, monolithic vision of the USSR is rigidly cemented in my mind, my relationship with that country is a bit more complicated. A year before I was born, in

1948, Tito decided to break with Stalin. To free Yugoslavia from Big Brother's iron embrace was a daring deed, considering that the USSR already held in her grip all the other communist countries in Europe. Literally overnight, the Soviet heroes who had helped Yugoslavia to get rid of the German occupiers became our enemies. So too did thousands of people within Yugoslavia, who ended up in labour camps, of which the most notorious was Goli Otok. Their only 'crime' was that in their confusion they were too slow to turn their backs on Comrade Stalin, as was now demanded by the political commissars. The destruction of these people's lives was the Yugoslav contribution to the Stalinist purges that had swept away millions in the USSR. Once the USSR was established as a dangerous enemy, anything coming from there was treated as a threat.

One of the consequences of this attitude for the great majority of my generation was that we did not learn the Russian language at school and showed no other interest in that country, either. It existed as a blank spot on the map of our interests. In the sixties, when we were teenagers, Yugoslavia was opening up to the West. We could travel to Great Britain, to Germany, or to France. Why would anyone want to go to the USSR? Later on, after Kruschev came to power, relations between the two states greatly improved, but in a way it was too late. We already had the translations of Alexander Solzhenitsyn's books; we had learned all about the death camps in Siberia, such as Kolima, and soon enough our own 'Gulag' literature appeared, which killed off any wish that might have remained to know the USSR better. Those who visited Moscow or Leningrad in the early seventies came back with stories about tourist guides whose task it was to spy on you; about people queueing for food; about the shortage of elementary supplies like toilet paper; about people who followed you in the street because they wanted to buy foreign currency from you, and this was the only way to get it.

This is how my picture of the Soviet Union was formed, the image of a wasteland with a thin crust of Siberian ice spread all over it. I knew enough not to have any desire to take a closer look. I had recognised what life there was about: poverty, despair, helplessness and booze; a smell of cabbage stew and rotten potatoes in the entrance hall of every apartment building; dilapidated walls; grim, peeling façades; dampness and the smell of hopelessness hanging in the air; people who, being constantly humiliated, had but one wish – not to be there, not to be who they were. Thanks to that, I understood the meaning of the word destiny.

Having a Yugoslav passport meant that you could travel both to the West and to the East, and the USSR was the only country in the communist bloc that I did not visit. Not only that, but I hadn't met a single Russian in my life until the late eighties. I could well say that all this was sheer coincidence, and it would be a tidy explanation, but, I now know that I subconsciously avoided it. Why would I visit somewhere that was the same as home, only much, much worse? In fact, I know that this was precisely the reason why some people from my country did visit the USSR. Besides the strong feeling of sympathy they had for suffering people there, they also had a rare chance to feel superior. I saw how this worked in other countries of the bloc whose citizens could not travel to the West. They would stop you in the street or in your hotel, knowing that you were a foreigner by the way you were dressed. All visitors from Yugoslavia knew this. They would fill their suitcases with jeans, stockings, female underwear, even chewing gum, and take them into one of the less fortunate neighbouring countries to sell their stocks on the black market, specifically to their guides, porters, chambermaids or waitresses, who would then probably sell them on. One could make a lot of money by doing this, but that money would be of no value outside the country you were in, so it had to be spent on the spot. This was the climax of the whole trip, the moment when a businessman, a delegate of some congress, a small party apparatchik or just a simple, poor tourist would kick away the traces and revel in the nightlife of Moscow, Prague or Budapest, drinking champagne, eating caviar and behaving like a king, even if only for a day or two.

This was the way we Yugoslavs profited from our comparative freedom. Our feeling of superiority came from a not very noble source, from the smuggling and selling of underwear. The deprivation of other people fed our vanity, especially in the USSR, because the people there were the most deprived and isolated of all. It was perhaps a kind of compensation for our own treatment in the West, where we felt humiliated by the wealth and the Westerners looked down upon us. Then it was we who felt inferior.

Living in Eastern Europe under communism, we were taught to compare ourselves with those who had less than we did, never with those who had more; to those who were worse off, never the better off. To compare ourselves with those who had a higher standard of living and more freedom would have been dangerous − we might have started to ask questions, perhaps even to demand the very same for ourselves. We were not free, we were not rich, but the consolation of our comparative comfort was reassuring.

It was enough to make a short trip and to convince yourself that others were living in even more desperate conditions – not enough milk, no detergent, no sanitary towels (not to mention a pair of jeans, a very important status symbol all over Eastern Europe at that time). It gave us a cheap thrill, but it worked. People told me how they had kissed the soil at the airport, when they returned from a visit to Moscow, and I had no reason to think that they were lying.

The word 'progress' was always one of the key words in the political speeches of my youth: look what progress we have made from a poor, peasant country; how many asphalt roads we have built, how many factories! Look how your life has improved! You are not starving any longer, your children go to school and have proper shoes, and everyone has electricity nowadays. No more tuberculosis or epidemics of other terrible diseases! Isn't that progress? And communism has brought you all that. It was true: the majority of our people lived in even poorer conditions before communism, and they still remember that. How could they ask for more? Only their children and grandchildren, raised in more or less normal conditions of life, could have expected more.

Because of all that I can not allow myself to be a tourist in my own past. I will never be a real tourist in the USSR: it would be too painful, too close to me. I realised that when I visited Romania two years ago. As soon as I landed at Otopeni Airport in Bucharest, I knew I was at home again, back in my past. I had only to breathe the overwhelming smell of cheap tobacco, heavy winter clothes and unwashed bodies, for all my memories to return. The policewoman at the border there had heavy layers of make-up on her face, too much blue eyeshadow, mascara, dark powder, red blusher. Her lipstick was too pink, too. An old woman with her head covered with a kerchief was sitting in a toilet with red tiles, selling pieces of a harsh, brown toilet paper. I felt heavy, as if a stone was tied round my neck.

When I arrived in the city, I saw women walking in white boots like they did twenty years ago in Zagreb; I saw stocky, dark men with moustaches wearing typical, tall, peasant fur hats. In the Hotel Dorobanti the ugliness of the steel-and-glass construction, the dirty tapestry and ragged furniture inside, made my eyes hurt from the absence of any kind of beauty. Then I visited a friend, a physician living in a one-room apartment, his bathtub filled with water because the running water does not reach the sixth floor in the building. He makes $40 a month. It was like watching an old movie, except that I was in it. I knew I took it all too personally; I could not distance myself from surroundings I knew all too well. It was a dreadful journey into the past, and I decided to spare myself a similar experience in the future. So I did not visit St Petersburg, or Moscow, for that matter. I was already tired, not only from Bucharest and Sofia, but even from Budapest, of my entire life under communism.

I guess I am one of those people who would like to finally reach Europe, whatever that means. And what is Europe, that Europe we yearn for? A Lithuanian in Timothy Garton-Ash's essay 'Journey to a Post-Communist East' gives a short and definite answer: 'Europe is ... not Russia!' It is brutal, it is ignorant; it is not even just to say that, but I like his definition of what Europe is and is not, at least for the moment.

In Zoe's Bathroom

I peed in her pink toilet, I washed my hands in her pink washbasin and touched up my make-up in a mirror above it. For a moment, I even considered taking a bath in her bathtub – pink, of course. Perhaps that was what every Romanian woman wanted to do, to enjoy the privilege of the Ceauşescu princess's bathroom on the first floor of the villa that used to be the family residence in Spring Street in Bucharest. I knew she would not approve of what I did, but with her parents shot dead, and she and her brothers stripped of all their possessions as well as their jobs, Zoe had no longer a say in this or any other matter. So, for a reasonable amount of money and on the pretext of filming something, I could do just that, pee in her toilet. A cheap thrill indeed.

When you enter the villa, separated from the street by a high wall, you pass the entrance hall with mosaics in marble and gold on the floor and the walls. Then you come into a white marble hall the size of a decent ballroom, with an elegant staircase leading upstairs into the living quarters of two of Ceauşescu's three children, son Valentin and daughter

Zoe. Her apartment consists of a *salon*, a bedroom and a bathroom, no kitchen (at least I have not seen one). While the *salon* and the bedroom are furnished in the rococo style, with silk wallpaper and heavy silk curtains, the bathroom is the place where their kitsch taste can really be seen. Much has been said about the opulence of the Ceauşescu family and its – especially the mother's – love of gold and marble, crystal and silver, evident in their numerous 'official' residences all over the country. But what is most striking about Ceauşescu's villa is not the opulence, but the bad taste. And the best example of it is Zoe's bathroom. All the fittings are in pink, while all the taps, the shower, handles and towel rails are gold plated. It is the combination of heavily designed golden taps that would perhaps not disgrace some Roman emperor's bathroom, and the two kinds of tiles, each in a different shade of pink and a different design – one, with an abstract geometric figure, on the walls; the other, forming the pattern of a rosebush on the floor – gives their taste away. Standing there, suddenly I had a clear feeling of déjà vu. Curiously, I felt as if I were in an American hotel, one of those places that like to present their guests with a particular idea of what is elegant and luxurious, as if some farmer from Iowa, more accustomed to growing potatoes, had arranged the bathroom to his taste. Which in fact is exactly the case with the Ceauşescus. Both husband and wife came from poor peasant families and had no proper education. For people like that, I could imagine that this was indeed a royal bathroom.

For Zoe's bathroom is not luxurious at all, but rather pathetic in its attempt to be luxurious. It is an ordinary, if spacious, bathroom of the sort you might see in middle-class family homes in the West. But when Zoe lived here, her bathroom was a statement of ultimate luxury, primarily because it functioned and was equipped with hot water, soap and toilet paper. It was the exception in Romania, which marked it as luxury.

I visited a friend living in a skyscraper in Bucharest. His little apartment does boast a bathtub, but often there is no water with which to fill it. Water, as well as electricity, often goes off. If you visited any state-owned or privately run restaurant – or any public toilet in the city – you would have the feeling that you had entered an underground world where civilized life had ceased to exist. This might well be one of the first things a newcomer notices upon arrival in this country: first the smell, then the look of its toilets. The famous restaurant Carul cu Bere in the heart of Bucharest, located in a beautiful nineteenth-century building they say was once a church, is no exception to this rule. Wooden carvings, ornaments on the walls and the whole atmosphere of a classical *bierstube* is preserved and the food is good, but the impression of quality is immediately distorted if you take the risky decision to go to the toilet. Closing the door behind you, you begin to choke on the sharp stench of urine as you desperately try to find a dry patch on the flooded floor. Needless to say, there is no seat on the toilet, but by the time you visit that famous restaurant, you will already know that such a thing is not to be expected. And then you have to pull a dirty piece of rope in order to splash the water. Soap is nowhere to be seen and toilet paper seems to be a completely unknown thing. There is not a single public toilet in Bucharest where you would find it.

How is this total absence of normal standards of hygiene to be understood? And what is the significance of this absence?

Coming from a former communist country myself, for a long time I readily explained the phenomenon of stinking, decrepit toilets throughout the communist world in the most obvious way. The primary cause was the dysfunctional communist system itself and its failure to recognise and fulfil people's basic needs, from milk to toilet paper. The second reason also fell into the 'what-communism-did-to-us' category, and had to do with the collective-property mentality. Since everything was collectively owned, no one was really responsible; no one was in charge, no one cared. Every individual was absolved of responsibility because he or she delegated it to a higher level, that of an institution. Someone up there had to make a decision for a chain to be repaired in a public toilet. And was a cleaning woman to be sacked from her job because she didn't sweep the floor? Of course not! The third explanation was low wages, and the attitude that engenders: if someone pays me so little, I will do as little as I can.

After visiting Bucharest, I must admit that I was wrong. The reasoning is justifiable as far as it goes, but it does not go far enough. I cannot find an answer to one key question: how could we ourselves stand that disgusting disorder? How could we daily pee in such places, without feeling ashamed of our culture. If there are no toilet seats in Romania, or they are far too expensive, perhaps stealing them is understandable. But why do we accept a piece of rusty wire or a rope to flush the toilet? Why do we put up with the smell? With no toilet paper? Why do we accept this filth as normal? There is no evident change in post-communist Romania. How come?

If you take a stroll in downtown Bucharest in the middle of the winter, all you can see is a sea of fur hats. This is the nation of fur hats: everyone, but everyone, wears them, old as well as young people. It is not because there is no alternative to this fashion, no woollen caps or hats, nor because they are too expensive: it is simply that a fur hat is a part of the national peasants' costume. Romanians wear fur hats because most of them moved into the city only recently and still cling to their old habits. This indeed is a nation of peasants, as are most of the ex-communist countries (though not all of them, with Czechoslovakia a case in point). Before the Second World War and the 'communist revolution', the majority of the population were country people. After the 'glorious victory' of communism, people migrated to the cities in vast numbers to fill the jobs created by the industrialisation of Romania. However, this did not mean that they instantly became urban people.

In the streets of Bucharest, the link between fur hats and personal hygiene suddenly became obvious to me. Anyone who has ever visited a village in the Balkans, for example, or, for that matter in the former Soviet Union, will know what I mean when I say that peasants simply have a pretty different idea of hygiene from that of townspeople. In the country you perform your natural bodily functions while working in the field, or in a wooden cabin in your yard. And what is regarded as 'clean' is certainly not the same in cities. But of course there is a big difference between the maintenance of a hole dug in the ground fenced by four planks and that of a water closet in a public place – or at least, there should be.

The communist crash course in urbanisation did not help the newcomers to change their habits, whether it was wearing fur hats, or using toilet paper and properly cleaning a toilet after using it. People were forced to jump from a village into a city, to make the giant leap from feudalism to communism, without the time or education to develop a civic society and all its values and habits, from the concept of private property to human rights, from democracy to toilet paper. This historical mistake has to be corrected now, but I am afraid that it will take time and that those of us who live in these countries in the post-communist era will have to wash our hands and use paper for many years, before we really stand a chance of developing democracy. One without the other – that won't work.

While the standard of Romanian toilets reflects the nature of the communist system of which it is a legacy, the absence of any improvement is also a warning for the future of democracy. People need time to change habits and to understand and implement new ideas and values, and one of the most difficult lessons is that of individual responsibility in every single area of life, from politics down to everyday practicalities. If we are to undergo yet another crash course, this time in democracy, the result will be more or less the same, and democracy will never become more than a new ideology, manipulated by our new leaders for their own purposes. For what else does this new democracy represent for us today? Is it more than a new ideology? It is still a mere dream, a new Utopian concept, a panacea, a tool for solving all our problems, from poverty to corruption, nationalism and war, in some unspecified way.

Moreover, most people have the wrong notion of democracy as a kind of natural calamity that has descended upon us, not something one has to understand, develop and work for. The values of a civic society must be created by its citizens, and one or two generations of peasants living in cities under a totalitarian régime had no opportunity to become citizens in either the political or the cultural sense.

Sitting in Zoe's bathroom, I understood that a civilised, democratic society has a very slim chance of immediately taking root in countries where a normal, clean bathroom with running hot water, toilet paper and soap was a luxury reserved for dictators.

To Have and To Have Not

One day on the staircase of our apartment
building in Vienna I encountered a neighbour
who lives on the first floor. I was on my way in
from the supermarket and was carrying an enormous
canvas bag full of food in one hand, trying to balance it
with two boxes of washing powder and a packet of nappies.
Andrea was surprised to see me dragging all this home, but
not as surprised as she was to see me with nappies. 'Why
have you bought those?' she asked me, perhaps thinking
that she had missed out on some important news. I
explained to her that I was taking it all to Croatia. The
nappies were for my friend's baby – they are much more
expensive in Zagreb than in Vienna. I was slightly afraid
that I would have to go into the nitty-gritty of Croatian
economics and explain that while people there are paid
only a fifth of the money Austrians earn, nappies still cost
more than they do in Austria. But Andrea was kind enough
not to inquire about the vagaries of the Croatian economy.
Instead, she popped into her apartment and reappeared
with another bag of nappies, no longer needed by her

daughter Fanny, who also came to the door to announce proudly that she did not pee in her pants any longer.

Croatia – war and refugees are perhaps what Andrea had on her mind when she brought me the nappies. But my friend back home is not a refugee. She has a steady job, but she simply cannot afford to buy nappies for her son, so I take some every time I go there. The other reason why I do this would be hard to explain to my kind Viennese neighbour: I feel *obligated* to my friend with a baby – and to my mother, my relatives and other friends living there, too. They have no money: they all make only between 350 and 500 US dollars a month and face a higher cost of living than people in the West. My friend with the newborn son has taken two jobs in order to survive. She was not lucky enough to get a job abroad – not that she ever expressed the wish to leave, but being able to live abroad is considered great luck by everybody. This has nothing particularly to do with her life or mine – it is simply a legacy of our history and the kind of society we used to live in. Yet this belief is rooted in our minds and we just accept it: those abroad are by definition better off, just because they are abroad.

But to tell the truth, Andrea's question made me think about all the things I buy to take to Croatia. I was leaving for Zagreb in a couple of days and as usual I had started to prepare for that trip by carefully composing a shopping list. From the supermarket I'll buy salami, cheese, chocolate, Nescafé, two kilos of ground coffee, washing powder, margarine, powdered milk, canned tomatoes, olive oil, fresh fruits – all cheaper in Vienna. Then I'll get some of those cheap stockings sold in packs of ten (handy for our teenage neighbour), underwear for my mother – perhaps even a nice pullover. I'll also have several prescriptions made up at the chemist's for my mother's neighbour, and while I'm there I'll buy multi-vitamins (also a good present, because they are very expensive at home). Then there are cosmetics, perfumes and other gifts. After passing the Austrian border I will inevitably go to the duty-free shop for whisky and good cigarettes – for the doctor who takes care of my family. Little by little, my car will be filled with goods, mostly presents.

Why do I do this every time I go back to Zagreb, regardless of whether I am travelling by train or by car? Why are my suitcases always full of such trivia? Only when I go from, say, Austria to Sweden can I say that I travel light. There is not much that is worth taking from one of these countries to the other, and it wouldn't occur to me to buy a perfume for a Swedish friend in Austria; in fact it wouldn't occur to me to buy her perfume at all, because prices don't differ that much. The most I buy is some smoked salmon as a gift for an Austrian friend, and even then only occasionally. But when I visit Croatia, or any ex-communist country – every time I go from the West to the East – I just have to take all kinds of things with me.

When I go home to Croatia I buy two kinds of goods: cheap food and household items, to save money; and expensive cosmetics, perfumes, soaps, drinks, cigarettes and sweets that I give away as presents, which takes up most of the money I have saved. Where is the logic in this? Am I trying to fulfil other people's expectations? And who is expecting presents from me? My relatives, my friends and people in need; the woman in the unemployment office who collects nice tin boxes; the nurse who likes to drink exotic kinds of tea; the neighbour who adores Austrian pralines, and another who is too fat to fit into a normal pair of tights. Going to Albania or Bulgaria it is the same story – except that where once I used to bring my friends useful things, like Tampax, now I bring them a bottle of French wine, good eau de cologne and the latest books. The times and the gifts have changed, but not their expectations.

These expectations are remnants of the old days, when those who could travel were really privileged. But now these goods can be found everywhere in Eastern Europe. The difference today is no longer the lack of choice, but the fact that very few people can afford luxuries.

It is this that makes me feel odd as I carry my purchases up to my flat on the second floor in Vienna. Without much reflection I obey the unwritten rules, and it is only when my Viennese neighbour asks why that I stop and think and ask myself the same simple and logical question. In the past the answer was obvious if you lived in one of those countries which forbade its citizens to travel to the West, for fear that everyone would leave (the last one out, switch off the lights, as the old joke ran). It was obvious even if you lived in a country like Yugoslavia, from which, from the sixties onwards you could travel freely, because you needed money to do that. If you managed to scrape together the money for a trip to the West, you were considered privileged indeed.

In those days, too, I would make long lists of things to buy, knowing that in the end I would have to decide between a book and a pair of shoes. Most likely, I would have had the very same frustrations if I had lived in the West, but that did not occur to me then. Like other Eastern Europeans, I naïvely imagined that living in the West automatically guaranteed you a certain standard of living and that such agonising decisions were unknown. The idea that I could be poor living in the West, perhaps unemployed; the fact that there is hardship and financial insecurity everywhere in the world, was beyond my imagination. If we are all poor here, they must all be rich. What else were we to think, when we knew that a person living on social security in the West was rich compared to someone with a job in a communist country? It was typical for a visitor from a communist country to think that poor people in the West had voluntarily opted out, rather than lost their job. They would have made it if they'd only tried harder. After all, I had seen in the countries I had visited – Germany, Italy, France, Great Britain – so many more opportunities to make money and have a decent life than there were at home.

But the myth of the advantage of living in the West has not lost its power since the demise of communism. Bringing presents is not only a social habit, the nice and expected gesture of someone who has 'been there', and a kind of proof that one has indeed 'been there'. There is also a psychological mechanism at work here, namely the egalitarian principle with which we all grew up. It reminds me of a little boy of about seven whom I met in Bucharest. My taxi had stopped at some traffic lights. He ran up to me and said: 'Speak English?' When I nodded, he stretched his hand through the open car window. 'Give money!' he said.

'Why?' I asked him, not really expecting him to understand me.

To my astonishment, he looked at me as if surprised by my stupidity. 'You have, I not have,' he explained seriously in his rudimentary English.

There was nothing wrong with the boy's logic. It was obvious that he had no money, otherwise he would not have been asking me for it. It was obvious that I had money, otherwise I would not have been driving around in a taxi. Even at his age he knew that there are basically two categories of people in a society: those who have, and those who have not. But according to the egalitarian principles of any communist society, those 'haves' should share with the 'have nots'. And because there is not much to share anyway, in the end that egalitarianism boils down to the equal distribution of poverty. At least it would in theory – in practice it did not quite work.

I vividly recall a big campaign in Yugoslavia more than ten years ago. It was organised by the government under the slogan: 'If you have a house, give back your apartment'. The idea was that those who had been able to build their own private houses should return their apartments to their local community, firm, institution, school, hospital, or whoever else provided them with their tenants' rights. The reason behind this campaign was, of course, the shortage of housing, and the guiding principle was the egalitarian one: you cannot have both an apartment and a house while others have nothing. This was the last serious attempt I remember to apply the 'you have, I need' principle, and it did not stand much of a chance. At that time, Yugoslavia was already swimming in quite liberal waters, developing a middle class and the framework for a free-market economy. It was hard to force people to give up their rights to apartments, and predictably, this radical Utopian idea failed. But it does illustrate how the concept of social injustice in a communist society works: those who have are exceptions, and they should feel guilty and ashamed – the others are entitled to have, too, because it has been promised to them.

Class differences were established immediately after the communist revolution, first by those who themselves promoted the idea of a classless society, that is the leaders or the 'red bourgeoisie', as Milovan Djilas called them. But the egalitarian ideology survived in different forms, for example in codes of social behaviour. The equation in my case looks like this: I live in the West, I have, therefore I am obliged to share. And I do feel obliged. I can't turn anybody down. I am still a prisoner of that logic. Moreover, in a patriarchal society, being married to a Westerner is considered a real achievement, perhaps a bigger one than making a career or a name for yourself abroad. Nobody would doubt for one moment that my husband is a rich foreigner – why in the world would I marry a poor one? My marriage also means that I have escaped the common destiny of my people: the war, poverty, insecurity, unemployment, disappointment, political confusion, low wages and the feeling that time is running out fast and you can't be certain if the future will bring anything better. As if living in the West has somehow vaccinated me against misfortune. Who would not feel guilty for 'escaping' from such a situation, even if my 'escape' is only an imaginary one? I certainly do. My friends certainly don't deserve any less.

There is only one thing that I seriously hold against my friends back home. They owe me something, too. It profoundly upsets me that I never hear from them. They do not call, they do not write. I know they have no money, and that international telephone calls are incredibly expensive because of the state monopoly of the system. It is accepted that people call you only when they want something – a place to stay, to borrow money, something to be sent or brought – or in a medical emergency. This I understand. But why don't they write? Stamps are not that expensive.

This experience is not unique to me: it is the general attitude of people in Eastern Europe. A friend living in Stockholm visited Belgrade in the summer. Afterwards, she sent letters, books, packages. Just the other day she complained to me that six months have passed, but no answer has come back to her. Being Swedish, she was puzzled. Had the letters and books arrived there at all, she wondered.

Of course they did. But it is she, not her friends, who is expected to call and write and send things and keep communication alive. They are *there*: they are in need, they are too busy suffering to respond. And if you don't accept this one-way communication, they'll tell you for sure that you have forgotten them, that you don't need their friendship any longer now that your life is a bed of roses. As if friendship would have anything to do with that.

So I call them. What else can I do? I do need them. My secret is that I do not like what they see as my great luck, I do not like living abroad all that much.

A Smile in Sofia

She wore a semi-transparent white shirt, and underneath I could detect her fine lace bra. When she leaned over towards me to take my passport, I could tell that she was using a good perfume, too. She also had a fashionable haircut and spoke good English. Yet, while I watched her, busy behind the reception desk at the Sheraton Hotel, I felt awkward. There was a strange, unfriendly air about her, and indeed about the three other receptionists there. She answered my questions briefly, almost brusquely, as if giving information was a favour rather than part of her job. And she did not smile. This was a sure sign that I was in Sofia.

Here, receptionists, bellboys, lift attendants and waitresses do not smile, not even when you are paying the $260 a night that makes the Sheraton in Sofia probably the most expensive hotel of its kind in the world. Behind their desk in the elegant marble hall with its distinctive Western flavour, the receptionists behave like princesses. Perhaps they almost feel that the hotel belongs to them. After all, until just recently, didn't everything here belong to the people? When a guest checks in, they look at him with an air of slight but unmistakable irritation, as if to say, 'Who are you? What do you want?' Moreover, they make it clear that you must earn any kindness, as a kind of personal reward. They seem too proud to smile, indicating to the guest (who already feels swindled for having had to pay for something he doesn't get): yes, we are here for you, but you won't see our smiles, because they cannot be bought. It seems that nobody has ever told them that they are here to serve.

If it is of any comfort to a visitor to Sofia, and I cannot imagine that it would be, it is nothing personal. It is the same story in every other public-service industry.

As I entered the Austrian Airlines office at the Maria Luiza Boulevard, the two young women there barely lifted their eyes from their computer screens in greeting. And instead of giving me an answer to my question, one of them just shrugged her shoulders and continued her private telephone conversation. 'Really? And then what did he say? . . .' After waiting for half an hour without complaining – by then I had become fascinated by this scene – I was given the wrong ticket. The error was corrected without an apology; indeed, the woman was angry with me for the mistake, as if it were my fault. Again, there was no recognition of the fact that the staff were there to serve the passengers, that they depended on us for their living. And not for a single moment did I detect even a trace of a smile on any of the four frozen faces of the Austrian Airlines employees that morning in Sofia.

At the Pirogov Hospital, where I went because I needed an urgent blood test, a woman in the laboratory started to shout at me as soon as I opened the door. Used to similar treatment in my own home country, I waited stoically for her to calm down. When I finally had a chance to explain to her what I needed and why, and when she realised that I was a foreigner, she decided to take pity on me – again, I was at the mercy of her whim. Everywhere, as a guest, customer or patient, I was treated in the same way.

But what opportunity have these people been given to learn a different approach? Where have they themselves ever seen a smile? Living their whole lives among sombre, grim faces tainted by the drabness of everyday hardships, they have had no chance to change their attitude overnight – especially if they do not even recognise the need for it.

My first plane trip to the USA, in 1983, was a PanAm flight to New York, and I remember it distinctly because of one episode. Just as we landed at J.F.K. Airport, a stewardess thanked us for flying PanAm – which was itself strange to my ears – and then she added: 'We are proud to serve you.' I was astonished. Proud to serve? How could anyone be proud to *serve*? I remember thinking as I left the aeroplane. It was a culture shock for me. I did not understand it at all. I was not familiar with any positive implications of the word 'serve'. In my East European vocabulary, it could mean only servitude, slavery, humiliation; something unpleasant and definitely negative.

I had a second culture shock as soon as I arrived in the States: the smile I encountered on entering any shop or restaurant. It was such an unusual sight, even if I quickly realised that the smiles were false – at least, that was what I told myself, not understanding at that time what an important part of any profession such courtesies are. The very next morning, I went into a bakery. The young mixed-race girl behind the counter smiled and said, 'So, how are you today?' I was confused for a moment. 'I'm a bit tired, I have jet lag,' I answered eventually, but before I had finished my sentence, she had already asked the next person at the door the very same question – 'my' question. She clearly had no interest in listening to the reply, much less in what it was. I felt embarrassed. I was still not quite aware that this was simply a formula, a code of communication that had nothing to do with interest, or truth, or my real feelings. The only proper and expected answer, as I soon learned, was: 'Thanks, I'm OK.'

But however meaningless it was, this quick exchange of a couple of conventional sentences was a vast improvement on the suspicious, unfriendly expressions on the faces of salespeople in my part of the world. So when someone greeted me with a smile and a 'Have a nice day!', I smiled back and said, 'You too.' I realised that this sort of smile was important, and that it looked nice, too.

But, as I have said, a smile is a rare thing in Sofia. You can wander from shop to hotel, restaurant or a café – private or not, it doesn't really matter – with as much of a chance of being smiled at as striking gold. Even the street vendors have not yet discovered the trick of charming passersby into buying a pencil, a chocolate or an orange. They look at you as if your sole aim in life is to steal their orange.

Sofia is a good place to observe the clash of the capitalist and the communist worlds because the superficial changes are so visible. The whole face of the city has changed in three years. There are many new privately owned shops selling food, clothes or electronic goods; there are restaurants and little cafés. Sofia is booming with a new spirit of private enterprise, from street stands to consulting firms. But they are not yet competing for custom; perhaps they don't yet need to do so. People here are hungry for all things new and Western and it will be some time before they become saturated with what is on offer and begin to discriminate between the ways in which it is offered. If you bear in mind that it is only yesterday that today's consumers had to bribe a salesperson to get a decent piece of meat or a pair of good shoes at all, the attitude of both consumers and those offering goods or services is much easier to understand. Unfortunately, it doesn't make it any easier to put up with it.

The more I looked around the new, capitalist Sofia, the more I thought of that American stewardess's words, and other courteous expressions I heard time and again in the States. Yet here a smile is a sign not of courtesy, but of the inferiority of the smiler. Capitalism might be here, but there is no understanding of its principles: the tenet that a customer is always right, for example, is unheard of. On the contrary, in this kind of facade-capitalism, the logic of the employees in the new enterprises is: 'Don't you for a moment think that you are better than us just because you have money! You may have money, but we have our pride.'

This attitude reveals two things. First, because these people have never had money, they are not aware of its power. It also shows what a confusing new process capitalism is. Instead of the fulfilment of the promise of an instant welfare society, everyone has to work hard, and only a few will get rich. And it does not guarantee you a job or security, or medical care or a pension. The idea of social justice, even if it means no more than poverty for everyone, is still strongly present here, if not politically, then morally, and there is a conflict between the new economy and the old communist values. People are not used to anyone having money, and they react to wealth with aggression or contempt. Money may not make you a better person, but it surely gives you the right to demand the service you are paying for.

When I remember our old history books, which depicted capitalists as fat men with cigars, while the workers looked thin and weak, as if they were just about to die, and our lessons in Marxism on class exploitation, not only of the working class, but also of the peasants, I can see where this 'non-smiling' culture comes from. The liberated communist working class has its pride and the basic concept of serving someone does not fit its new ideology or its egalitarian principles. This is why it cannot be a part of the code of communication here. Indeed, it equates with humiliation. The same goes for a smile. Not so long ago, a smile could provoke distrust. Why is that person smiling? Does it mean that he or she is happy – how is that possible, with all this misery around us? A show of happiness was a reason to suspect a person – at best it was considered indecent. If under communism everyone was unhappy by definition, then it was logical that no one smiled, that it was not a tool of any trade.

In the 'non-smiling culture', the laws of the new system, new values and behaviour have not yet been fully grasped. True, in the 'smiling culture' not everyone smiles, and many do it only professionally, but the difference is that smiling is legitimate; it is legitimate to feel happy or just good, and to express it with a smile.

In Sofia, I became aware that in the new circumstances the absence of what we take for granted as habits or social customs reveals crucial misunderstandings, even signs of a culture clash. To overcome this, it will take more than the introduction of free-market economy, private initiative or even democracy. When I go to Sofia, and see someone smile, for me that will be a sign of real change.

Leaving Sofia, I took a taxi to the airport. The driver of the old Lada did not even look at me. He muttered his price with a cigarette hanging from a corner of his mouth. The car was vibrating from the loud disco music. His radio was left on, constantly emitting a terrible noise. But I did not say a word; I did not dare to. Obviously I was to consider myself lucky that I was permitted to use his private taxi as public transport. The message came over loud and clear: 'This is my car, and I do what I please. Understand?'

Yes, Mr Taxi Driver; yes I've got ya! I thought.

The Pillbox Effect

When I first saw the row of five military pillboxes just outside Rinas Airport near Tirana, my reaction was: this is it, this is Albania as I have read about it and expected it to be, a country turned into a communist prison. Of course I knew this – everyone did. But the surprise lies somewhere else, in the sheer physical presence of the pillboxes. You see that first row and you think, OK, perhaps an airport needs to be protected like this. The second row, only 20 metres away, is perhaps justified. But then you notice the third, fourth and fifth rows, all of them 20 to 50 metres apart. By now you have stopped counting and started to think that this cannot be real. If there are so many of them in such a small area, the whole country must be literally covered with pillboxes! No one can be that crazy, you think. Your imagination runs wild as you try to envisage hundreds of thousands of these concrete monsters protruding from the ground like some strange, poisonous kind of gigantic mushroom, transforming the whole landscape into a badly painted set for a theatre of the absurd.

It was bad enough for me that my prejudgement was confirmed, but what really gave me the creeps was that the reality here is even more fantastic than I had imagined. Enver Hoxha built an estimated 600,000 to 1 million military pillboxes in Albania. At that time, for the cost of two of them you could have built a two-bedroom apartment. Communism in Albania was obviously expensive – but the revolution, which began in 1991, was not cheap, either.

Once my eyes had got used to these strange objects, these monuments to the past, something else caught my attention: the metal constructions on the roadsides which looked almost as bizarre as the pillboxes. It took me some time to work out what they were: these were the greenhouses where the Albanians used to grow vegetables for export. They were not easily recognisable because they were smashed. What remained were the iron frames, partly torn down and partly bent out of shape, but still standing. As I looked at the sheep eating salad mixed with weeds, I noticed that the ground was covered with what must have been tons of broken glass. It felt like being in some kind of science-fiction movie, like *Mad Max II*. There was something deeply disturbing, deeply apocalyptic about this waste landscape and the visible destruction. Who had done it, and why?

I asked my Albanian friends. It had happened during the revolution, in 1992, a friend explained. People smashed everything they could – they even destroyed factories, for example the big bread factory on the outskirts of Tirana. They wrecked and plundered shops, hospitals and schools, in towns as well as in remote mountain villages. My friend told me that he had seen a mob demolish a greenhouse in about two hours. Some people took the water pipes or metal frames to make fences or to use for repairs in their homes, but mostly it was pure vandalism. There was no way to stop them, my friend said, and no one dared to try, neither the leaders of the new Democratic Party nor the police. This was one of the saddest things I have ever seen, he concluded.

This is where the Albanian revolution diverges from those in the rest of Eastern Europe. Such annihilation did not happen anywhere else. Communist monuments were removed, yes, and here and there a party building was attacked, but not schools, not factories, not greenhouses. Is it possible, I asked myself, that people here were so foolish that they were unable to understand their own interests and needs? Why was there such an amazing level of violence? Or is this how they understood freedom: as freedom to destroy?

But I don't think that the Albanians were foolish when they did this, but they were naïve and full of hatred. To understand what happened in Albania, you must keep in mind the pillboxes. Their only purpose was to create and perpetuate fear. If you live surrounded by them, when freedom finally comes, that fear turns into hatred and aggression. You could even call it the 'pillbox effect'. People were not smashing up a greenhouse, they were smashing up a greenhouse co-operative, the symbol of collective or state property. Even a school or a kindergarten represented the communist state, whose power to oppress was based on those pillboxes. The violence was an expression of a wish to completely erase the past, even the material aspects of it. It was as if the Albanians could thereby exorcise the evil on a grand scale, as if a better life was waiting for them just around the corner. I can almost hear them shouting: 'We don't need anything old, because we'll get everything new and better. This is what freedom and democracy is all about!'

But where did this promise of a better life come from? As soon as I reached the outskirts of Tirana, I discovered the source: the television screen. The shabby, dilapidated two- or three-storey houses all look as if they are falling apart, but each house has several satellite dishes on the front. In Tirana you can feel how important television must be for people if they are ready to invest a considerable amount of money just to have the satellite dish necessary to watch foreign programmes. This is where the vision of the future life came from, as well as the idea of what revolution is all about: it should bring not only a change in political power, but also a better standard of living. In my opinion, more than anything else, television advertising is to blame for the revolution. They create the false expectation of instant fulfilment of all desires. If only you buy this product, drink that drink, drive this car, you will be as beautiful, rich and successful as the people you see on the TV screen.

One evening in Tirana I sat and watched an Italian soap opera in a friend's house with her two teenage daughters. As the ads flashed over the screen, interrupting the programme, the faces of the two girls would light up with joy. Each of them would repeat their texts, which they knew by heart. That evening, it seemed to me perfectly possible that the way to a better future in Albania was to get into that magic box and disappear to the other side of the screen, like Alice going through the Looking-Glass.

Who still remembers the exodus when tens of thousands of Albanians went through terrible humiliation just to reach their own Wonderland? Did they really know what was waiting for them there? I doubt it. Their desperation to leave Albania was real enough, but their naïveté was acute. That naïveté is the most fascinating and moving aspect of the Albanians. No other country in Europe was isolated to such an extent; no other country was 'protected' from reality by a million pillboxes. Without any communication with the outside world, it is not surprising that they believed in the beautiful images of the outside world. People here told me that under Hoxha you could end up in prison for pointing a TV aerial towards Italy. Hoxha was aware of the danger of the political propaganda underpinning this visual seduction. The ultimate price of isolation and naïveté was high: a kind of self-destruction. It was as if Albanians believed that a nation or an individual could start its life from point zero.

The hope of a new life, it seems to me, begins with bananas. Right across from Hotel Dajti was a young man with long hair, dressed in jeans and sneakers. At his street stand, a cardboard box on the pavement, he was selling a few bananas, a Mars bar, a cigarette lighter, a couple of packets of Marlboro cigarettes and some chewing gum. I watched him standing there every day. It did not seem to me that he did much business, because even if his 'shop' did not look very European, his prices certainly were. Not many people could afford the 'luxury' items he was selling. But the fact that he sold only a banana or two each day, perhaps not even that, did not seem to worry him much. After all, what else could he do in a country where almost the whole population seemed to be unemployed and living on humanitarian aid (and between 1992 and 1994, the aid provided by the European Union amounted to $420 million), but stand there and hope to sell one banana, then buy two, then sell two, then buy four, until ... well, until he could afford a kiosk.

In Tirana, a kiosk can be any box with a roof, provided

that it is big enough for a person to stand, or even sit in it. It could be made out of corrugated iron, or pieces of metal found, usually, in the garbage. It could also be a car trailer or a plastic container. And as I watched that guy in front of the Hotel Dajti, I knew that his dream was to have a kiosk of his own. In Albania, it represents a quick way of getting rich. Strolling around Tirana, I had a feeling that the face of the city would soon be completely changed, with kiosks outnumbering the concrete buildings.

These kiosks literally grow up overnight and already more than 2,000 of them appeared in the two years between 1992 and 1994 in Tirana alone. If you have a relative in Italy, Turkey or anywhere abroad, who will put up some money, if you have access to the 'channels' to obtain smuggled goods, and if you know whom to bribe in the state administration to get permission for such a business, you can have a kiosk in the space of a day. Perhaps I am mistaken, and people do have enough money to buy a hamburger, a cup of coffee or a banana, but even if they do, who is really getting rich? Certainly not the young man with the street stand dreaming about it. At best, he will be employed by someone to sell in the kiosk instead of on the pavement. But the invested money will go back where it came from. As it is virtually impossible to tax the kiosk owners because of corruption, no money will go to the state. And if there are no taxes, there will be no investment, no new jobs, no roads, no pensions, no health insurance. My guy in front of the Hotel Dajti will probably be happy, because he has a job. But with this kind of small-business economy, the state is likely to remain poor.

What Albanians are enjoying now is the theoretical possibility of getting rich, which is very much like the theoretical possibility of buying a bottle of whisky or a good perfume, when you don't have enough money even to smell it. In a way, they are living in an illusion of a capitalist society, as well as with the illusion of freedom or democracy. The extreme poverty of the country makes this all still a dream. Albania looks to me like a dormant, dreaming country, a child that has not yet learned how to take care of itself. And no one can tell how long it will take it to recover from the long disease of isolation, poverty and despair.

Money, and How To Get It

In the summer of 1994, my Swedish friend Jan, a television journalist, visited the Czech Republic. He was making a programme about the concentration camp in Theresienstadt and this was his first visit to Eastern Europe. Another friend, a Czech, volunteered to help him. Jan was in need of an interpreter and a secretary for a couple of days, so Vladek introduced him to a young student willing to do the job. Marta's role was simple: she had to make a few telephone calls, to arrange meetings with various people and accompany Jan and his crew, all in all, three or four days' work. It was agreed that Jan would pay her 1,500 German marks in cash, plus her expenses. To Jan this seemed very expensive, but as time was short he had little choice, so he accepted. Besides, Vladek explained to him that this was the market rate in Prague nowadays.

The girl, in her black leather mini-skirt and fishnet stockings, was not dressed properly for the job, but Jan did not comment, since he was not familiar with customs or fashion habits in the Czech Republic and did not want to offend her. During the three days she worked for him, Jan discovered that Marta's English was not good enough and neither were her secretarial skills up to the standard he expected. In short, she did a rather lousy job. He told Marta that he was not satisfied with her performance and that therefore he could not pay her the full amount they had agreed upon. Marta was stunned and Vladek, who had arranged the job for her, was surprised, to say the least. Jan had the money, so what difference did it make to him how much he paid? The money belonged to the television company, not to Jan personally. Jan found himself in a very unpleasant situation. Not only was he displeased with the job, something which he had expressed clearly (which, as he learned later on, was not the custom here), but neither Marta nor Vladek seemed to understand what he was talking about. Of course he was talking about the principle of not paying for something that had not been delivered, and he explained that 1,500 marks for such work done properly would be considered a lot of money in any Western country. He did not like to be cheated – who does?

Marta insisted that the job had been done. She was puzzled that Jan wanted to discuss the quality of it, and that this was somehow connected to the amount of money she should be paid. What did it matter that 1,500 marks was a lot of money in some other country? She couldn't have cared less how much it was worth somewhere else, because this was the 'tariff' here.

It was like a dialogue between a deaf person and a blind person. The girl went so far as to actually try to threaten Jan in an indirect way. She said that her boyfriend would be very disappointed if he found out that she had got less money than she had been promised, as if her boyfriend were some sort of pimp. In the end, she even started to cry.

'I need that money,' she said between sobs. This was her very last argument against the stupid foreigner who had not only tried to swindle her, but had also humiliated her. Being a gentleman, and conscious that he was trying to work in another world, where market forces mean over-pricing, but not adequate services, Jan paid the girl the full amount. But he was bitter, if not insulted. Did people in Prague think that, just because he was a foreigner, he was also a millionaire.

Well, in a way, yes, they did. I understand his feelings on being confronted for the first time with this catch-as-catch-can attitude towards foreigners. I still keep two taxi receipts from that summer of 1994. For journeys of exactly the same distance, two hours apart, I paid 100 Czech crowns in one direction and 200 on my way back. Yet I was not exactly cheated. The system is more sophisticated than that. Both times I saw the amount on the meter with my own eyes and got a receipt, so officially everything was all right. As well as being outraged, I was curious, so I asked the driver (the expensive one) the reason for the difference. He shrugged his shoulders and gave me a very short answer: it was just different companies. Of course in almost every country there are different companies, but their prices do not usually differ by 100 per cent. The reason is simple: no one would ever use such a taxi company and it would soon cease to exist. In Prague, the locals, of course, know very well which company is affordable. The expensive ones obviously 'specialise' in foreigners.

The next time I had to use an expensive taxi company in Prague, I did not speak English. I used my Croatian language, which is similar to Czech. When the taxi driver realised that I was a Croat, he took pity on me (the war) and as a result I paid a 'normal' fare. I can't say that I saw him fiddling with his meter, but he must have performed some trick. From then on I spoke only Croatian in Prague and I have to say that I was treated differently. At least no one assumed that I was a millionaire. However, I didn't do the same thing in Budapest, and so I let myself in for the same kind of trouble.

At the railway station I took the first taxi in line and it cost me 2,700 forints (roughly $27) to reach my destination. This is exactly what one is not supposed to do, a friend told me later. In Budapest, there are only two reliable taxi companies that will charge you a normal fare. First ask a driver how much your journey would cost and then you haggle, because you can be sure that the original price will be outrageous. If it still seems too high, you just go to the next driver, and so on – they are used to that. Sure enough, I noticed the difference. A couple of days later, when I returned to the station, I paid four times less for approximately the same distance!

It seems to me that taxi drivers in Budapest understand the rules of capitalism in a negative way: as the absence of any rules, except for the familiar overcharging of tourists; perhaps even as the absence of any law at all. Prague taxi drivers who charge you 'only' 100 per cent more are angels compared to their Budapest counterparts. I noticed that neither police nor any state authority can do anything about this law of the jungle, which is a frequent topic in the press. Taxi driving is considered private enterprise, and fair competition is an alien concept there. There is certainly not a proper organisation to regulate this matter. But there is something else about it, something much more fishy: anybody will tell you that taxi drivers are a well-organised, rich mafia with a lot of power and the ability to 'oil the wheels' where necessary.

But if an extraordinarily expensive taxi ride is your first touch with the new reality in, say, the Czech Republic, you are in for more surprises. For example, for the same grade of hotel room you will be charged double the price paid by the gentleman filling in the registration form next to you at the reception desk who is chatting amiably to the receptionist in the Czech language. Why? Because he is a Czech citizen and you are a foreigner. Yes, you are taxed for being a foreigner, which here still equates with 'rich'. This rule was set up long ago, during communist times, in every Eastern European country, and despite the changes in ideology, many of them still keep it, for an obvious reason: money. You might think that such plain discrimination on the basis of your nationality (a kind of nationalism?) would have disappeared because a free-market economy does not differentiate between locals and foreigners. But here it does. If you are aware that such a discriminatory tradition already exists, it is easy to see that taxi drivers have only stretched this principle a bit. If you are charged double for a hotel room, why not for a taxi ride, or anything?

No wonder foreign visitors feel cheated at every turn. Try, for example, to have a car repaired in Prague and you'll see how much more you'll have to pay just because you are a foreigner. And if you have foreign plates, don't be surprised if you find your car slightly damaged at the back, with a typed note under the windscreen wiper saying: 'Dear Sir, I ran into your car last night because you were parked in a wrong place. My car is greatly damaged, so I expect you to send 400 German marks to my bank account, number . . . .' This is exactly what happened to a friend of mine three years ago. Foreigners feel cheated because they are cheated. By their language, they are clearly marked as another category of people, the category to be ripped off.

This attitude can be partly explained by the old double standards combined with the newly discovered possibilities of making money without scruples to compensate for the suffering of the communist years. As in Marta's case, it is again a kind of 'you have, I need' principle. But surely it is also based in part on the concepts of money and work, and the relationship between the two. On his first visit to the former communist world, my Swedish friend expected professional service, respect for some basic principles such as punctuality and diligence; at the very least, appreciation of the value of money, as is the case in Sweden. What he found was a communist attitude towards jobs, money, professionalism, foreigners and principles. In his view, one has to properly sweat for 1,500 German marks – money does not grow on trees. But how can people who have never seen any connection between money and work know that it does not grow on trees?

This attitude towards money and work reminds me of a popular game, *šibicari* – the shell game – or street betting, a practice which goes on in various forms all over the world. In almost every town you can see guys standing on the pavement surrounded by a group of people watching them fiddle with a small paper ball and three empty matchboxes. The man quickly turns the three boxes around while the other people bet on which box the ball is in. It is impossible to win – the only person who does is the partner of the guy with the matchboxes. It is not surprising that these men try to trick people, but it is amazing that there are those who are willing to give it a try and lose their money. It is not big money, but that is not the point. The point here is to make some quick money with the help of a trick.

This is exactly the attitude towards money in the post-communist world of today. People watch smooth operators moving around in a much more sophisticated way than the three matchboxes, but, as in the shell game, they can see a tiny new elite pulling tricks to get hold of money from the black market, real-estate speculation, smuggling, the manipulation of privatisation and shares, corruption, money-laundering or some other mafia-style or just plain criminal business. No one is getting rich by working. People think that there must be a trick to getting the money if only they could find out what it was, and they are right. The work ethic is non-existent anyway: no one ever got rich by working before, only by climbing up the party ladder, or pulling another kind of smart trick. In the experience of ordinary people, you work a little and get a little money. If you worked more, you would not get more money, so why bother?

We have brought with us into our new system the mentality of forced labour: you work, but you get nothing out of your job; no promotion, satisfaction, pride, respect – or money. So you do not invest your energy or hope in your job. On the contrary, you try to spare your energy, ideas and knowledge to use elsewhere, if possible in a second job, preferably performed during the working hours of your first job. You act as subversively as you can, and at the end of it, you get a pittance. And the rewards are precisely the problem today, because now you have to work harder for the same pitiful $40 (the average monthly wage in, say, Albania, Romania, Bulgaria or Serbia). In these conditions it is impossible to develop a work ethic, to consider the quality of your performance or to treat equally those who have no money (the locals) and foreigners, who, in this context, still appear to be rich.

Yet another psychological element of the contemporary

– or rather, persistent – attitude towards money is the absence of a future. This is essentially inherited from communism, too. Then there was no future, only a 'better future', that is, an improvement on the present. What that improvement consisted of people knew by heart: more control, more fear, perhaps more food or a colour TV set, a refrigerator, a car at the best. The prospect was not very exciting. When you cannot plan, invest, advance in your career or your education, travel freely, move to a better job or plan a better future for your children, that is not much of a future. So the little money there was was both easily made and not much needed.

This made life predictable. There was not much to expect and one got used to it. Indeed, when 'future' sounds like just one more empty catchword, people are rightly afraid that instead of improving slightly things could get even worse. Yet that very predictability gave people a feeling of security, of protection. It is a paradox that what people today miss the most is the security they have lost with the fall of communism: jobs, pensions, social and medical security, maternity leave, sick leave. As a result, you don't invest, build or save in the name of the future. You just grab what there is today, because it might not be there tomorrow. So future is still non-existent in practical terms; it is distant and blurred and not yet to be trusted. A restaurant owner explained this to me very simply when I asked him why he didn't lower his prices, since his restaurant seemed pretty empty. He told me, 'I have to take all I can today, because I don't know what will happen tomorrow, whether I will have the same chance again.' People still find it difficult to understand that this is not their last opportunity, that it would be better to work with the future on their minds, that ripping off someone means he might never come back again. But you learn only by experience, and five years is just not long enough for that.

Incidentally, just as I wrote this, the Czech Republic passed a law giving customs officers at their borders the right to check that a tourist entering the country has a minimum of $20 per day. Interestingly, the Czechs have resurrected this practice from the old days. Communist or not, it is not bad if it serves your interests.

In *The Financial Times* of 20 October 1995, I read: 'The former director of the Czech Republic mass-coupon privatisation scheme, Mr Jaroslav Lizner, has been jailed for seven years for corruption and fined Kc 1m ($38,000). Mr Lizner, who also headed the securities registry, was arrested last year outside a restaurant in Prague after he had been given a briefcase containing Kc 8.3m in cash. He was accused of taking the bribe to fix a stock deal.'

Could this be just another coincidence?

The Trouble With Sales

So, I have money at last. Not big money, to be sure – but then, everything is relative. If you have lived your whole life on the edge of survival, having some cash in reserve is really something. For me, it is an achievement. But it is in itself a problem. What should I do with my money?

If, ten years ago, someone had told me that having money could be a problem, I would probably have burst out laughing. I would have told that person, 'Give it to me, I know what to do with it!' I would most certainly have known how to spend it then. Spending was the only thing you did with money; it was what money was for. Today I realise that I did not understand a thing about money.

How could I? The little money I managed to save, I spent easily, with no hesitation. There were always more things I badly needed than I could afford to buy, so there was no point whatsoever in even trying to save up – I would never have been able to save enough. I know this does not sound logical. When you have only a little money, the sensible thing would be to save it in order to have more.

But save it for what? For a capital investment? Those times were long gone. In the mid-sixties, when the standard of living and the level of income in Yugoslavia had been higher, it was possible, for example, for my parents to build a weekend house on the coast. Of course, this was a consequence of Tito's successful policy of borrowing from the West, which finally amounted to a foreign debt of more than $20 billion dollars, but at that time, who cared about the foreign debt? However, my generation struggled to survive. I had no hope of saving any money from my monthly wage – no one did. In the mid-eighties bank loans for buying apartments or houses no longer existed; inflation was skyrocketing, so even if you had had any money, putting it by would have been fruitless. In short, the whole economic system worked against saving. It was a period of decline, and there was nothing to be done but to spend money on the things you could afford, like food, clothes and travel. This is why I had no problem spending the peanuts I had.

From time to time I dared to imagine what having money would be like. To my eyes it was like living in a consumer's paradise, a huge self-service where you could shop until you dropped. But a single glance at my unpainted walls, worn-out furniture and ten-year-old Renault 4 car – not to mention the thought of things I desperately needed – instantly cured me of such unhealthy fantasies. I realised that, if I ever had some money, I would first need to repair my apartment. But it was in such a bad condition that I couldn't see myself ever saving enough. All I could do was close my eyes and go on, patching up the house a little here and there and buying the odd luxury I could afford – books and magazines, perfumes and cosmetics, dresses. I had more dresses then than I have now.

When a friend from abroad visited me in the mid-seventies, he noticed that women in Zagreb were dressed very elegantly and wondered how it was possible on the little income they had. But at that time the cost of living was still low and spending the little surplus money was the only fun we had. The result was that we all looked and behaved as if we were rich. We developed an easy-come, easy-go attitude to money.

But even spending what we did demanded a strategy. Travelling abroad, I could afford to buy clothes only in sales. I am not bothering to discuss shopping in my own country, because there was not much to buy there in the first place. Sale goods there were real rubbish. The things in sales in Graz or Trieste were rubbish, too, but there was a difference between our rubbish and the rubbish produced abroad. It was all cheaply made, it's true, but sometimes, if you searched hard enough and were lucky, you could find cheap things that looked expensive.

God only knows if these sales, or *sconti*, in Trieste were genuine sales. I always suspected that they were not, and I felt cheated. I thought then, as I do today, that shop owners had discovered the magic attraction the word 'sale' held for us poor Balkan suckers. Piles of underwear, T-shirts, shoes, dresses – anything labelled 'sale', drew us like flies. There was also a ritual in the way you shopped: you went in the morning, early enough to be able to check all the usual places (Giovanni, Standa, Ponte Rosso) early, because, you told yourself, you would be able to snap up the 'bargains' before anyone else. You would not even look at the 'better' – that is, normal, shops. What would be the point? The *magazini* we regularly visited were stuffed with the same cheap crap, but prices were lower and saving a few thousand lire meant you could afford to buy yet another pair of jeans or sneakers, which is what it was all about.

Years and years of such habits have moulded my attitude towards shopping and indeed to money in general. Not my taste — taste is something you develop independently of your resources. Taste, when you have no money, is about what you do with cheap things you buy, how you wear and combine them. But to this day, as soon as I see the magic word 'sale' and spot something reduced to £9.99 in England or $19 in America — or 99 German marks, 199 Swedish crowns, 199 Austrian schillings — any small sum in any currency, in fact, I have to investigate, if only to see for myself what they are selling — kitchenware, sheets, towels, detergent — even if I'm actually shopping for shoes. It is a compulsive act for me, I have to look to avoid the feeling that perhaps I'm missing a good opportunity. Of course, I end up buying ten T-shirts (they will always come in handy), three pairs of espadrilles (I need them), and a dozen pairs of panties I can't resist, just because they are cheap. All at the cost, as I explain to myself as soon as I am back at home, of 'no money at all'. What is more important is that buying so much for so little, gives me a sense of satisfaction.

This is an art, I think, proud of myself for a moment. But no, it is not, and deep down I know it. I am aware that the T-shirts will fall apart after two washes and the espadrilles after I have worn them for a week; the elastic in the panties was already going when I bought them. Buying junk is not an art, it is only a sad necessity. Or, in my case, a bad habit that you can't get rid of, like smoking. For Christ's sake, times have changed, everything has changed, says my husband. You make some money now. You don't live in communist Yugoslavia any longer (well, that one makes sense, Yugoslavia doesn't even exist now). You can buy what you want. I try to explain to him that I can't, but I am afraid he does not quite understand me. After all, he is a Western European.

Besides, he is one of those men who buy the most expensive things he can find in order to be sure that they will last several generations at least. So what do I do? I lie to him. I buy something in a sale and add a zero or two. It is a little white lie, and I suppose that most men would be happy if their wives cheated them like that, rather than the other way round. But he is not happy. He wants me to get used to the new, post-communist reality, that is, to buy quality goods. As he has known me only a couple of years, he is not aware of my shopping history. He does not grasp that I do not care too much about quality. Look, I am used to things falling apart, I explain to him. I don't feel guilty when I buy them, because I am not throwing money away by paying too much. But that is exactly how you do throw money away, he argues. Maybe, I say, but I haven't learned that lesson yet. I need more time.

But my problem is worse than I dare to admit to him. If I buy something expensive, I do not dare to wear it. It feels unpleasantly expensive. I am afraid it will get crumpled or dirty, or that I will destroy it in some way. Two years ago, I bought a nice two-piece by Kenzo. And although I know how good I look in it, I wear it only on very special occasions, for example when I met the Swedish Queen. But how many times in your lifetime can you expect to meet a queen? I also have an absolutely elegant Armani dress, so elegant that when I think about it now I wonder how on earth I brought myself to buy it. I must have had an attack of amnesia. But I have worn it only a couple of times. As a result, it will soon be out of fashion, and then I will regret having bought it even more.

Perhaps it is even more disappointing for me that not even my daughter understands my love of sales, even though she grew up under communism and moved abroad only recently. Nevertheless, she spends all her money without any complexes or feelings of guilt, and not in the sales, to be sure. I doubt that she would even understand what I am talking about. She has been affected in a different way by her communist background. She is hungry for things she used to lack, and has turned into a compulsive buyer. She works to earn money to spend, because buying makes her happy. And from my perspective this, if anything, is the definition of a consumer.

From time to time, I play a standard psychological trick on myself. When I really want to buy something, but do not dare to, I take my daughter shopping with me. Then I have a good excuse (because obviously I need one): she talked me into it. I remember buying a Laura Ashley dress some years ago. I guess it took me an hour to try it on, take it off, try it on again. I was very hesitant and could not decide, because it was not exactly a cheap dress, and the argument that I needed it for a particular occasion did not really persuade me. Then my daughter said to me, have you noticed how that woman looked at you with envy? This time, my vanity won. But she hates going shopping with me. An ordeal, she calls it. A paradox is what I call my own attitude to spending.

For a year now I have had a gold Eurocard. As an Eastern European, I am absolutely fascinated by it, especially by the idea that I can use it in any foreign country. Imagine, just anywhere – in shops, hotels, restaurants. It is not that I haven't seen a credit card before. I even had one, an American Express card. But it was issued in Yugoslavia, so it was a kind of Yu-Amex. It could be used only in

Yugoslavia, for the obvious reason that the dinar was not a convertible currency. Even so, it was great fun to own it and I remember how proud I was when it arrived in an envelope in the mid-eighties. It felt as if a whole new world was opening up in front of me, just as I had seen in the Amex advertisements abroad. Of course, no new world opened up, but I could at least get a taste of consumerism. If I walked down the street and saw a pretty dress in a shop window, I could go in and buy it without having the money to pay for it. I could take it away immediately and pay a whole month later. This was a real thrill. I understood why Americans say that plastic is fantastic.

I mercilessly used my old Yu-Amex, especially at the beginning of the inflation crisis. It was a great thing. You could beat inflation more easily, which was no small matter considering that by the late eighties it had reached 2,000 per cent. I used the card for everything, even food in the supermarket – until they introduced a different system. Then you had to pay your bills every two weeks and, worse, a 30 per cent penalty if you were late.

My gold Eurocard gives me a very different feeling. It's more for looking at than using. There is no longer 'funny money' behind it, but real money, hard currency that I must work hard to earn. Expenses are automatically deducted from my account, so there are no thrills from trying to beat the system. The gold Eurocard doesn't give me the freedom I fantasised about, instead it serves more as a kind of insurance, proof that I can pay if I find myself in trouble; if I need to spend money, not if I merely want to. To tell the truth I have used it only once for shopping. I do not dare to use it for such trivial pursuits, just because it is gold, I think. Not even the card has helped me to successfully bridge the gap between the two extremes of spending when you have not and not spending when you have. A paradox, again.

I sense something else in my new asceticism. It has to do with changed social and political reality. Clearly, I was not in a position to become aware of my own paradoxical attitude towards money until times had changed, communism had collapsed and we all started to live according to the new economic logic of capitalism. Only then did I realise how much I am influenced by the communist system, its poverty and its morals, under which I grew up.

I first started to make a bit of money in the post-communist era. To my own surprise, my first impulse was to start saving for future black days. It is hard for me to explain this exactly, but I recognise a gut feeling, a yearning for security. Before, that kind of security was guaranteed to me by the state. I knew I would get a pension; I did not need to think about it, and even if that money was not enough, at least it was there, and I could count on it. But a state is no longer responsible for all our needs and we must learn how to think about the future in an entirely different way. Many new democracies still claim that they are welfare states, but in practice they cannot afford it, for the simple reason that there is not enough money any longer. It means that I have to provide some kind of a pension for myself. The change, in psychological terms, is a drastic one.

In fact, perhaps it is the first time that my generation has had to think about its future at all. The idea that our future depends entirely upon us, upon our capacity, ability, and so on, is a bit scary, but challenging, too. The problem is that we can all see that the system supporting this idea does not really function. The post-communist economy seems to be a peculiar conglomerate of private enterprises, suspect privatisation of state-owned property, organised crime, and plain corruption. When you see it everywhere around you, you cannot really believe that the future depends upon your ability, upon yourself. Ability to do what? To steal?

So I have to stop spending on everything I now consider unnecessary or luxurious, goods I would have bought before with uncomplicated joy. A lost pleasure? Maybe. But let's remember that our small pleasures were not based on real work and real money, but on another kind of cheating. There was the whole so-called 'grey' or illegal economy to which we could help ourselves: working for quick cash, or using your working hours to do something else which would bring you an extra income. Now, if you are lucky enough to have a job – because many people don't – your wages are not earned easily. And once you have money in your hands, you don't necessarily rush to spend it; instead you try to make it work for you. When you are poor, you spend, and when you start making money, you want to make even more. We have all read about this in books, but only now do we have direct experience of it.

As far as I am concerned, this asceticism, or love of sales, or feeling of insecurity, can only be a problem for my generation. The fall of communism happened in the middle of our lives. The younger generation behaves differently. They have a much more entrepreneurial attitude: they open small businesses, borrow money, invest. They struggle, but they can't afford to be afraid of the future. They are improving their lives and expecting to do even better. This is because they started to work under the new conditions, and these are all they know. They suffer because of the lack of a safety net, but they don't feel it as a loss.

Also, they are not yet bothered by the question that troubles me: how *much* money do you need to save in order to feel secure? I am afraid that, by now, I know the answer: this amount is not attainable. If you are over forty, you cannot hope for any large increases in salary, you can only inherit it. The few who will inherit a fortune will not change the picture for the rest of us. So we are back to the idea that a society has to function in such a way as to guarantee people's minimum social and medical needs. This is the only way in which every individual can feel safe. Until this new Utopia materialises, I have no choice but to continue shopping in the sales.

My Frustration With Germany

Whenever someone asks me what I think of Germans, I remember my history textbooks from primary school and a drawing depicting German soldiers fighting Tito's partisans. The German soldiers had tanks, aeroplanes and machine-guns, while the partisans were armed with only a few primitive-looking guns. This drawing represented what we at school had to memorise as 'the unequal battle against a much stronger enemy'.

When I went to primary school in the mid-fifties, the Second World War was not yet forgotten and our textbooks were full of German, Italian, partisan and Chetnik soldiers, just as textbooks in some other countries are probably full of kings and princes and dukes. But even before I started school I had encountered Germans in the stories of people around me, in phrases like 'When the Germans attacked us', 'When we fought against the Germans', 'When I was wounded by Germans'.

In the first grade we learned that Germans were occupiers, that they had bombarded towns, burned villages and killed innocent civilians all over Yugoslavia. Such lessons from our teacher were usually accompanied by an emotive drawing of a burning house in our textbook. These history classes were considered very important and in order to make us remember them, the teacher would take us to the cinema to see movies about the war, the partisans and Tito: *Neretva, Sutjeska, Kozara, The Landing in Drvar.* In those films blond German army generals with cold blue eyes wore perfectly ironed uniforms. Because they shouted throughout, regardless of what they were saying, they seemed unable to speak normally. As a consequence, their language sounded pretty frightening. The partisan heroes in such movies called the Germans *Švabe*, which was meant as an insult; sometimes they even called them *Švapske svinje* – German pigs – and I could understand why.

We saw the same few films over and over again every school year, and every time they made me cry. I cried because of the unbearable cruelty of the German soldiers. Even today I can vividly remember one scene from *Kozara*. A partisan soldier is hiding in a hole under a road along which the German army must pass. The Germans are searching the terrain metre by metre, looking for partisan shelters, by sticking their bayonets into the soil. The partisan hero holds the wooden lid above him with one hand, while with the other he keeps a small child's mouth shut to prevent it from crying and giving away their hiding place. When I close my eyes I can still see the knife stabbing the hero's hand while he silently clenches his teeth. In that moment my heart stood still, and I felt as if the knife were stabbing the palm of my own hand – and the movie was not even in colour!

But the strongest impression of the Germans I got as a

child was from a poem by Desanka Maksimović which describes a true event, the death of a whole school class executed by German soldiers in Kragujevac. We recited this poem every November at the commemoration at school of the state holiday, the Day of the Republic. I guess that all the pupils imagined themselves being taken to be executed, together with our teacher. Later on, a movie was made based on this story, giving schoolchildren an even greater opportunity to identify with the murdered class.

With this influence, how could I feel anything but fear and hatred towards these horrifying Germans? It might seem an abstract fear and an abstract hatred today, but for a child of seven or eight in the fifties, it was as real as it could be. When, in the fifth grade, we had to choose a foreign language to learn, only a few pupils dared to pick German. All those who had chosen English looked down upon these poor kids, who had been forced to take German by their parents. The only language group in the school smaller than the 'Germans' were the 'Russians' – this was in 1959, and the Russians were also pretty unpopular, though for different reasons.

The extreme hostility towards not only the German army, but the German people in general, continued until the mid-sixties, when workers from Yugoslavia went to Germany as *Gastarbeiter*, or guest workers. Soon there were between 1.5 and 2 million people working there. I suppose that at that time the history textbooks must have been changed and, most likely, different movies were being made, too. Children of that generation started to watch Walt Disney films, and that was good. How could they believe that Germans committed all those horrible crimes during the war, when their fathers worked in Germany and sent money home from there? How would they have felt if they thought that their parents worked in the land of the enemy, in constant fear for their lives? So, for the *Gastarbeiter* children, Germany was Paradise on earth. And it became so even for the rest of us, because the money earned in Germany went to the most underdeveloped parts of our country, to Bosnia and Dalmatia. In no time at all there were beautiful villas built everywhere.

Yugoslavs became better and better off, partly because of the workers in Germany – as well as bringing marks into the country, they solved the unemployment problem at home – and partly because of Tito's habit of borrowing money from all over the place. Suddenly, only twenty years after the war had ended, those who had relatives working in Germany were considered the lucky ones. The fact that those workers lived there in extremely difficult conditions was carefully hidden.

These were the days when the first tourists visited our coast. We could not offer them much more than the beauty of nature, but that seemed to be enough for them. By the mid-seventies they were visiting us in millions, and even the smallest fishing village had a hotel, an exchange office, a restaurant and everything else required by a developing tourist industry. Needless to say, most of these tourists were Germans. In spite of the prosperity they brought, we still called them by the old, insulting name, *Švabe*.

The first time I saw real Germans in the flesh was at the seaside, on a beach. They were fattish; their skin was very white and after a short time in the sun, it took on an ugly pinkish colour. They had very weird habits: they went into the water with plastic sandals on their feet; they would swim on a lilo (which I then saw for the first time); they covered their skin with all kinds of oil, milk and cream with exotic names like Piz Buin or Ambre Solaire. Then, in the evening, they would drink a lot of beer at the restaurant. All in all they seemed more peculiar than dangerous to me.

But by then, the childhood hatred of the Germans was already forgotten. My generation had grown up with our eyes fixed firmly on the West. Our ideals were a career and money, not this or that ideology. To us, the Germans represented Europe, the world, money, the consumer society, freedom, travel, enjoyment – all of the things that were so difficult for us to reach. From time to time, watching them and remembering my childhood, it would occur to me that although the Germans came out of the war as losers, they had more of everything than we, the winners, had. This would have been confusing, had it not been for communism. Otherwise we would have been equal, I tried to convince myself. I suppose I needed such an explanation because of my pride: it hurt a bit that everything in Yugoslavia at that time was cheap for them – quite good hotels, dinners at nice restaurants, drinks – and that they could easily afford what we could not.

But now that period of admiration mixed with envy has passed as well. If you have seen a bit of the world, a pot-bellied German tourist with a Mercedes car and some hard currency in his pocket cannot impress you any longer. In the eighties, Yugoslavia developed into the cheapest package-holiday destination in Europe. The German tourists who visited our coast now were ordinary workers – factory workers, car mechanics, hairdressers and secretaries. Finally, we could show our disdain for them as we sat in the shade, sipping our coffee and spending the money we had made from them. The profit of millions of German marks from tourism created a decent standard of living for Yugoslavs and, what was even more important, brought us social peace. Our wartime enemies had now become our favourite milking cows.

But another unpleasant complication with the Germans was to resurface. During the war Croats had a special relationship with Nazi Germany. The Independent State of Croatia (NDH) had been a German puppet state. While Yugoslavia was profiting from tourism, this inconvenience was easily forgotten, but after the country fell apart, the government of the newly independent Croatia immediately re-established firm links with their old friends. Germany was the first country to recognise Croatia, and Croats and Germans became best friends again. In fact, the Croats were so grateful to the German ex-minister of foreign affairs, Hans-Dietrich Genscher, that they even erected a monument in his honour on the island of Brač. Today the connection between the two countries is so close that it sometimes seems that Croats can't wait to be colonised again by Germans – it would at least give them a short cut into the European Union.

My frustration with Germany and the Germans, from the Second World War to this one, might have changed, but it did not disappear. From my childhood textbooks, from movies and from life itself I concluded that, regardless of whether they are your enemies or your friends, Germans are always big and strong. I also have to admit that, from the perspective of a citizen of the Republic of Croatia, and especially because of its past, I admire them. For it is only now, when I can see that my compatriots are not able to do it, that I can understand how much strength was demanded of a nation not to erase its fascist past.

The Importance of Wearing a Uniform

On Sunday, 22 January 1995, the alleged Serbian war criminal Željko Ražnatović-Arkan threw a lavish wedding party in Belgrade. The marriage took place in an Orthodox church and the bride was dressed in a long, white lace dress and veil. Arkan wore a uniform. Not a proper uniform, because he is not entitled to one: he is neither a real soldier nor an officer in the regular Serbian army. He is the commander of a paramilitary unit called the 'Tigers', but that day he did not put on his standard camouflage battledress and black woollen cap, in which he has been photographed a million times during the war in Croatia and Bosnia.

No, for this solemn occasion he chose something more sophisticated: the old Yugoslav royal army officer's uniform. Of course, he has no right to wear this one, either – he was not even born when such uniforms were in use – so he decided on a copy of it with some decorative additions; a kind of historical costume, so to speak. He might just as well have chosen the uniform of Lord Nelson or Napoleon. In that costume, Arkan looked not only pretentious, but also pretty pathetic. Apart from betraying his terrible taste, it turned the whole wedding into a charade of operatic proportions. But he did not seem to care that to some it resembled a performance in a provincial theatre. He cared only about the majority, and he knew that the majority would see it differently.

So why did Arkan choose to dress in an historical uniform, though a uniform nonetheless, for his wedding? If he had been a real Royal Army officer, one could explain it away as tradition. But things being as they are, especially with the war in Bosnia going on, one could see it as his wish to gain some respect, some sort of dignity: the uniform suggests that he is an officer, when in fact he is only a criminal, an alleged mass murderer. Arkan is searching for legitimacy, and this formal dress, though only a copy, was designed to mask everything that he and his paramilitary troops have done during this war. He wants to suggest visually that all the crimes he committed were perpetrated in the name of patriotism, on behalf of the Serbian nation. He wanted people to recognise him as their hero, but to do this they needed to be able to identify him instantly as a Serbian. His camouflage battledress makes him look like just another soldier, or a member of any paramilitary group in any country. If he wore a civilian suit for his wedding, he would just look like any civilian. He had no right to wear the contemporary Serbian army officer's regular uniform, so he had no choice but to put on a uniform, one that people would connect with their own history, with the tradition of honour and gentlemanly behaviour generally associated with the officers of the old school. It had to be a uniform, because in the Balkans, a uniform above all evokes respect – the kind of respect that is born out of fear. Arkan wanted to evoke this, too.

And he was right in his choice, a uniform, any uniform, suggests just that. Arkan is not without a certain experience. When he campaigned in the elections in 1992 as the president of the Party of Serbian Unity, he appeared on a poster dressed in an elegant civilian suit. Then he wanted to suggest to potential voters that he was a peaceful, well-off citizen and a modern businessman who 'keeps his word', as the slogan went. This image was not very successful, however, and he got a disappointingly small number of votes. It is not surprising, for Arkan's real authority is based on exactly the opposite image – on the fact that the seat of his power is his 'job' of ethnic cleansing, as a commander of his paramilitary unit. He has money, all right, but so do many others; what others do not have is a paramilitary uniform that gives them the licence to kill in the name of the Serbian nation. Arkan apparently learned his election lesson well, realising that, if he wanted to be respected by the Serbs, it had to be through the power of his uniform; symbolising his 'service' to the nation. Without his uniform, his soldiers and his arms, Arkan would be nobody.

There is some justice in the fact that he does not have today's Serbian officer's uniform. It proves his impotence in a way. Because he is not a real officer he had to improvise, to reduce himself to wearing a copy of an historical uniform, a pseudo-uniform. An officer's uniform should imply a certain code of behaviour. It should signify that you have discipline, that you obey orders and that you respect the rules of warfare. A uniform should also perhaps restrict the beast in every human being in times of war, imposing a sense of order when it seems that all rules of human behaviour have been abandoned – even if this is very hard to say of the Serbian officers today. Look at General Ratko Mladić.

And in Arkan's case the uniform clearly could not have this last function, as he is notorious for his 'war' against the civilian population, of which no real officer could be proud. He insisted on all this symbolism nonetheless. But his choice I see as a supreme irony: as an imitation, it does not oblige him to observe even a modicum of ethics. Arkan's interpretation of a uniform is typically Balkan: above all, it represents the abuse of power.

The point of a uniform, as the word literally implies, is to dress people so that they all look the same and individuals don't stick out. For centuries this second aspect has been particularly strong in the Balkans. Far from being just anyone, it is only when you put on your uniform, acquired from the state, that you become somebody; only then do you have the chance to stick out of the crowd.

As a child, I was fascinated by the change that took place when my father dressed up in his colonel's uniform. He would become a different person, he would raise his voice, his posture would become stiff. He was no longer my daddy, but a strange, arrogant man. He was more important in his own eyes, and in the eyes of everyone around him too: he became powerful just because he wore that uniform. It gave him a different kind of authority, the authority of an institution. That institution, the army, stood above individuals, above all people. The army was not there to defend people, to serve them – what it was supposed to do if you didn't live under communism or a military dictatorship; it was there to make communist party rule possible. The military was part of their 'insurance policy', and everyone knew it. But even a conductor on a train, or a postman, or a doorman was aware of the power of his uniform and he would take every chance to exercise it.

In the poor, country areas of former Yugoslavia, when a

family had sons, one would be sent into the police or the army and the other to the church, to become a priest. The family was then relieved of the costs of their upbringing and their education, which would be shouldered by these institutions. For many young men, this was the only way out of the misery of a peasant's life and a chance to see the world beyond the hills around their homes. On becoming a soldier or a policeman, the young man would get a uniform and a pair of good shoes – usually the first suit and shoes he'd ever had. That immediately made him superior to his peers, who did not have the privilege of wearing a uniform (a sign of a direct connection to the state, and thus to power) and especially a solid pair of shoes. From nobody, he would at a stroke become somebody.

In times of war the soldier's uniform is even more significant. At about the time of Arkan's wedding early in 1995, a Croatian newspaper reported quite a different story about a uniform, an incident involving a soldier of the Croatian army. On New Year's Eve this soldier had been hitch-hiking to the front line a few kilometres away. For two hours, every car just passed him by, avoiding him like the plague, according to his own description.

Then one car passed with its lights on full beam. The soldier had the impression that the car was trying to run him over, as he explained to a journalist later on, and he threw himself to the roadside. In a fury, he grabbed a stone and threw it at the passing car, breaking the window. The car returned, and four men got out and started to beat up the soldier. One of them shouted that he had worked in Germany for that car. Who was going to pay for the broken window pane? 'Who do you think you are?' the man went on. 'Do you think that you can do what you like just because you are a soldier?' The soldier complained later: 'If only I'd had a bomb with me.' Luckily, he did not.

In the newspapers, this incident was presented as an extremely humiliating experience for the soldier, as a sign of disrespect for what his uniform stood for – the newly independent Croatian state, the war against Serbian aggression, patriotism, and so on. The fact that this soldier picked up a stone, hit the car and damaged it was brushed aside as totally unimportant, a gesture that shouldn't provoke anybody to react so brutally. The soldier thought he had the right to respond in such a way to a civilian who was not only ignoring him, looking down upon him, a Croatian soldier, but was even deliberately trying to hit him. The soldier was offended, and as he saw it, this gave him every right to administer 'justice' in the way he did. He felt that not only he personally, but, more importantly, his uniform and all it symbolised, had been insulted.

When the police finally arrived, the owner of the car shouted at them, asking them how they could permit such behaviour from the soldier. So the policemen responded in the way they felt their own uniforms entitled them to do: they hit the soldier.

Everybody concerned took the law into their own hands. The four civilians were defending private property; the soldier thought that love for the homeland and respect for the uniform that represented it was more important than private property. If a Croatian soldier, on his way to defend his country, breaks your car window, or anything else, you are supposed to put up with it. His uniform is there to deter an aggressive reaction. When the policemen appeared, they wanted to demonstrate the power of their own uniform in establishing law and order.

This small event clearly illustrates the clash of values in post-communist society: on one side is a uniform and its traditional association with ruling, rather than serving; on the other the defence of private property. What made the soldier think that he had the right to throw a stone, even to toy with the idea of throwing a bomb? Surely it was not simply his character, even if this played a part, but his uniform. Afterwards, he completely justified his own behaviour, interpreting the incident as a humiliation of the whole Croatian army. He even claimed to be protecting the four men in the car from a revenge attack by his father and his friends – 'Please don't mention my name. My father could get mad and kill somebody. My fellow soldiers from my brigade would kill the car owner, too. These fellows should thank God that I am a Croatian soldier who thinks of consequences.' Evidently, he saw no contradiction in concluding that, had he not been a goodhearted and responsible fellow himself, 'those nasty civilians would be long dead'.

The broken window was only a broken window, and patriotism, in this case the respect of civilians for his uniform, should take precedence over private property. 'I am not guilty!' the soldier insisted all the way through the interview.

This kind of logic could emerge only from the special tradition of the significance of uniforms prevalent in the Balkans. It is to be hoped that this incident will be an isolated one, rather than an indication of the general attitude of uniform-wearers in the new Croatia. Yet even nowadays Croatian soldiers break into civilian apartments on a regular basis, kicking out the inhabitants if they are of the 'wrong' nationality. This is criminal behaviour, pure and simple, but our state, allegedly ruled by law, does not have much to say about this 'right' exercised by men representing it.

The people themselves are, as always, simply afraid of uniforms. For the moment, uniforms are winning the battle for supremacy with private property. Their legitimisation of aggression, brutality and crime, no longer in the name of communism, but now on behalf of nationalism, is here to stay for some time.

And this brings us back to Arkan's wedding.

A Premeditated Murder

This is a story about anger, about fear, but most of all about the feeling of helplessness.

It was a public execution. On Saturday 25 February 1995, on Strossmayer Square in Zagreb, a row of innocent victims was executed, slowly and deliberately. They stood in silence, waiting for their turn. First, a few executioners in blue overalls would surround one of the victims, each holding an electric saw in his hand. Then the process of killing would start – and it was a process, because the victims were old, some of them well over a hundred years of age, with huge trunks that were difficult to cut up. It took at least half an hour to murder just one of them.

The sound was the worst part of it. There was no wind, and in the ghastly silence you could hear first the high-pitched noise of the electric saws cutting through the wood with great strain, then the cracking of frozen branches as the tree started to fall. Finally came a dull thud as it hit the ground, a sound like an immense sigh, shaking all the surroundings and making people tremble, too.

The victims of this brutal execution were the maple trees

in the very heart of Zagreb. Attacked by people, the maple trees, naturally, could not defend themselves. Only other people could have defended them, but instead they stood there in silence, watching. It was a crisp winter's day, yet a crowd of people came to look, pushing their fists deep into their pockets and jumping up and down to keep warm. A woman covered the eyes of her child, as if she didn't want it to see the crime. An old man cried. Most of the people looked incredulous, as if they could not believe what they were seeing. Some shrugged their shoulders and just passed by. No one looked happy, not even the workers performing their slow and unpleasant duty.

This is what happened on that winter morning, or rather, what did not happen: a group of citizens stood and watched a murder and did nothing. There may have been enough people gathered there to stage a small demonstration, but no one dared say a word, let alone do something that might look like a protest – blocking workers, hugging the trees, making a speech, singing – anything. They stood passive and immobile, almost like trees themselves. Or like future victims. Why did they do nothing?

There are three squares with parks in the middle of Zagreb. They cover several hundred metres, from the square of Ban Jelačić in the north to the old Austro–Hungarian main railway station in the south. From the air they look like a beautiful green oasis, something like Central Park in New York, and they have the same function. Collectively they are called Lenunci's Horseshoe, after the name of the architect who planned them in the last century, and they are a part of the city's very identity.

The first trees to go were on Tomislav Square, next to the station. One day the square simply awoke naked, stripped of its green coat. Young trees were planted to replace the old ones. There was no public discussion about this act at all. Not that the citizens did not see it – it would be hard to ignore such a thing. But it was a *fait accompli*, and it seemed that the destiny of the city centre's trees was not as important a problem as the refugees, the bad economy or the local elections.

Or was it something else that prevented people from reacting? Then came the public execution at Strossmayer Square. Now, only one more park, Zrinjevec, at the very north, remains to be 'put into order', after which the whole centre of Zagreb will look different.

The official explanation is always the same. As the mayor of the city said, two days after the trees were cut down in Strossmayer Square, they were old and sick and there was a risk that they would fall down and hurt somebody. It is a busy city and, of course, this couldn't be allowed to happen; it should be prevented in time, or a severe accident might occur. His explanation sounded plausible. The only problem was that it was given *post-festum*, after the murder had already been committed. This key fact was not picked up either by the press or by any citizens' organisation. The few discussions that did appear in the newspapers concentrated on aesthetics. The young trees planted in place of the old ones were not to be allowed to grow 'untidily' any longer; instead they were to be trimmed in the French style. Did it look better to have trees with 'untidy' tops, or neatly trimmed in the French way? It is probably not necessary to point out that this argument was conducted exclusively among the experts.

It became apparent that this 'improvement' to the city's appearance had been decided upon long ago, back in the eighties, at a time when there was no money to fund it. Now the money had been found, and the plan fitted nicely into the concept of giving the city centre a new identity. It also coincided with the new city administration and the new government of the Croatian Republic, which wanted to leave their own visible imprint on Zagreb. The City Institute for Space Planning formally signed the order for the tree execution, which means that the explanation that these trees were diseased was merely an excuse for killing them. The real reason was to make the new plan possible. If all the trees really were sick because of pollution, they could have been saved with today's technology. Ill or not, they could have been gradually replaced by the new ones, but that would have scuppered the whole idea of a neat 'new look'. In fact not all of them were diseased: this would have been evident to anyone who cared to glance at them as they were cut down.

Still, this is not the most important aspect of this case of premeditated murder. That lies in the secrecy and silence of the operation. Amazingly enough, the whole operation became widely known only through the 'Letters to the Editor' sections of the press – amazingly, because in the old days such letters addressed issues that journalists were not supposed to touch. This practice has continued in the main daily newspapers, controlled by the government, for the same reason as it was used under communism; that is, to censor certain subjects. Two full pages of such letters are about the only place you can find polemical writing in the official press. This is not to say that letters pages are totally free from manipulation or control, but still there are some issues that are discussed only in this form. Such was the case with the trees.

These letters revealed how the city administration operates. They had a plan for the appearance of the city and they hired experts, but they did not discuss the plan in public. It was not that the plan was a huge secret, but they simply do not have the habit of launching any kind of public discussion, not even among experts themselves. In their arrogance, it did not occur to any of the officials, from the mayor downwards, to consult, ask or inform anyone else – least of all the citizens of Zagreb.

Let's remember that we are not talking about private property here, but about public amenities that every citizen has the right to use, and perhaps about which even to express his or her opinion. But the city administrators have not changed their thinking or behaviour because nothing has prompted them to do so. They are used to imposing a 'solution' (cutting down) to a 'problem' (untidy-looking trees, some of which were diseased). They are all accustomed to the way things worked under the previous system, where no city bureaucrat would have dreamed of publicly discussing any sort of plan, much less delivering reports on, say, the public money spent on such a project.

Why change anything now? The administrators and the experts behave as though they are not responsible to anyone but the mayor, who gave them their jobs and who is paying them. The mayor of Zagreb has evidently not learned yet that he is responsible to the citizens, the taxpayers whose money he is spending. In short, those in power are still operating pretty much as before – from above. Yet, if you mentioned democracy to them, they'd be all for it in theory.

Obviously, some concerned citizens dared to telephone the newspapers, which were then forced to ask the authorities for an explanation. But the city administration and the experts are not the only ones to be blamed. The citizens themselves behaved as if they had no say in the matter, much less the right to make demands. But, as the newspapers' letters pages later revealed, they really were angry. True, they could not show that anger before the officials acted, because they did not know about the plan. But where was that anger when the trees were killed? Why didn't they show it then? When I asked my friend, who saw the whole thing from her window, she said: 'We could not do anything.' Another friend told me that the authorities, had planted new trees, so the tragedy was not that big. To me, it sounds like a justification of his own inactivity. The truth is that, when it happened, everyone was surprised and shocked. One letter perhaps best summarised the feelings of the Zagreb citizens about the tree execution: 'We are completely helpless and without influence.'

Again, it seems strange that nobody felt seriously offended by the insult to their elementary democratic right to be informed before something like this happened, not when it was too late. But afterwards no one demanded that someone took responsibility for the public interest. In the first place few people saw it as a problem. Those who did were most probably aware that the Croatian democracy is not the most developed in the world and that an insistence on information, explanation, responsibility, and so on would be less than welcome to both the authorities and to other not-so-daring citizens. So, why bother? The cutting down of a tree is nobody's personal problem and does not directly interfere with one's life.

The protection of one's own interests has been everybody's sole priority until only very recently. Everything that was public was considered state-owned or state-ruled – 'they' should take care of 'it'. Now, suddenly, there is such a thing as public interest. But it is difficult for people to grasp that in the end, it is *our* interest and *our* problem, and *our* citizens' right to act in the name of it. But how do you define a common, public interest, and how do you fight for it? It is a new issue, because it is something that could become an issue only in a democracy, where one can actually do something – start some action, organise a pressure group or lobby, and influence public opinion. This seems self-evident, but only to those who don't live here. Here people don't think in this way; they are not prepared for it, either by their political leaders, or by their media. They do not necessarily make the connection between a unilateral decision to cut down the trees in their city and democracy. But how else can you learn to put democracy into practice? It is not an abstract concept; it will not develop if nobody is willing to take a personal risk to move it onwards.

If the people of Zagreb did make that connection, they should have tried to stop the workers and their electric saws. Most probably, the trees would have fallen down anyway, but the citizens would have done their duty. Only several months later, another square in Zagreb – that of Petar Preradović – lost its identity. However this time the citizens organised a petition which, in a single day, collected 8,000 signatures against this 'urban genocide'. It was all in vain, of course. But people did stand up for their ideas. They did protest. And that makes all the difference in the world. It brings hope for the future.

A King for the Balkans

His Royal Highness the Crown Prince Alexander of Yugoslavia stood in a park in front of a microphone, holding a piece of paper in his pudgy hands. He was excited. This was his first public appearance, the very first time he had addressed his subjects as the crown prince in the middle of his capital, Belgrade. The crowd of tens of thousands of people stretched as far as he could see. At first he heard a murmur, for the crowd was no less excited than he was, followed by a tense silence, full of expectation.

Prince Alexander could hardly believe that this was happening, that he was standing here, in Belgrade, in front of all these people, who had come to greet him and to listen to their long-absent, almost forgotten prince. Only a few months previously he had been an ordinary businessman in London, the city which his father, King Peter, had chosen for his exile as a young man in 1941. Alexander had been born there in 1945 and had spent his whole life abroad without much prospect of ever returning as king of Yugoslavia. What hope for the throne could he nurture as long as Tito was alive? Instead, he had set out on a business career. His first wife was a Spaniard and his second a Greek. He did not have any contact with his potential kingdom whatsoever; in the first place he was forbidden by the communist government even to visit it. Of course, he was aware of the existence of that beautiful, if somewhat wild homeland of his in the Balkans; he had read Rebecca West and he was aware of being a Karadjordjević. But to be a prince without land did not interest him very much. He was a practical man, lacking the need for this kind of fantasy.

Then the impossible happened. Communism collapsed, and there he finally was, His Royal Highness Crown Prince of Yugoslavia. Perhaps even a king one day, who knows? His royalist friends, in London and in Belgrade (suddenly, he discovered that Belgrade was full of royalists), told him that there was a real chance of him regaining his throne. At first, Alexander did not really believe that such a possibility existed, but after a while he succumbed to it, especially since his wife, a commoner, had embraced the idea of becoming queen. He decided to take his chance, and started to prepare himself to give interviews as if he was already an important figure, to offer his opinions on the latest political and economic issues, to speak about the future of the country.

Anybody in his place would probably have done the same. After all, hadn't the most improbable event – the downfall of communism – already happened? Could one rule out a further miracle? Alexander thought that it wouldn't hurt him to try. He had nothing to lose, everything to gain – maybe even the entire kingdom. Well, perhaps not the entire kingdom, since Slovenes and Croats were already giving very clear signals that they had no intention of remaining within Yugoslavia. Nevertheless, he would establish himself as a serious pretender to the throne, placing his name on the list of those royals who hadn't given up hope of taking over the country. And if the big plan failed, he thought, a bit of advertising in the world's media wouldn't be bad for business.

As he stood there, in front of the crowds, he became aware that he was not used to so many people, so much attention, so much hope. He felt that his palms were sweating. 'Dragi Beogradjani,' he began. Alexander had courtesy enough to address the crowd in the Serbian language, even though he did not speak it at all – that was a measure of how much he really believed he would take back the throne one day. He had rehearsed the speech, and was determined to make it appear as natural as possible. However, his accent was so bad that his words were not understood at all. Yet this did not seem to matter much. As soon as he opened his mouth, the crowd cheered and applauded him frantically. The language was not nearly as important as his presence – the fact that here was their Crown Prince, finally addressing them.

What really mattered was that he was back, and with him, the whole royal spectacle: the solemn ceremony in the Orthodox church with a lot of prayers, gold shining and candles flickering at the altar, the tolling of church bells, the singing of the old anthem 'Bože, Spasi Kralja', the tears, the bows and curtsies, the aristocracy. You could not say that Prince Alexander looked like a prince from a fairytale, or even a tabloid newspaper, or Hollywood movie. He was not tall, or elegant, or handsome. There was nothing noble about his heavy, stocky body, his short fingers or his face, the face of a slick car dealer. But he was the Crown Prince, and he generated a feeling that the past had been restored to these people waiting for him to speak, who had been forced to live for fifty years without any rights to that past. HRH the Crown Prince Alexander Karadjordjević of Yugoslavia brought it all back that day, just by saying, 'Dragi Beogradjani'.

What is wrong with this picture? I thought, watching the whole ceremony on TV. Was it really possible that these people wanted a monarchy in 1992? If that was the case, then what was the revolution of 1989 all about? I myself thought, perhaps wrongly, that it was all about the attainment of democracy. But now it seemed to be more complex than that, at least in the Balkans. Out of nowhere, royalists appeared in growing numbers and with visible aspirations. Moreover, this was not the case only in Serbia, but also in Bulgaria and Romania, as well as in Albania, all of which were kingdoms before the Second World War. King Michael of Romania had been forbidden to visit his country by the new government, because of the fear that his presence might provoke the same sentiments as Prince Alexander's was doing now in Serbia. Out of the blue, a trick of history had suddenly put the four successors to the thrones in these Balkan countries, who had spent most of their lives waiting, in a position to play serious political roles.

A king in the Balkans? One might have thought that communism had succeeded in erasing every memory of the past, of the monarchies, that is, since it was its intention everywhere to convince people that history started with communist rule. It is true that not many of the Balkan nations had good memories of their monarchies. Indeed the Serbs did not, as in Yugoslavia before the war the monarchy had turned into a bloody dictatorship. Besides, all four nations were more or less poor peasant countries and the majority of their people had lived better under communism than monarchies. They had had more to eat, more educational opportunities and their health had improved. But what is absent from history, what is forbidden or repressed, often turns into a myth.

The explanation for the desire to re-establish the monarchy in the Balkan countries is however not to be found exclusively in reminiscences of the good old times. It is more strongly rooted in the nature of the communist system itself, as well as in the period of confusion and insecurity following the breakdown of communism. If before people had lived in a historical vacuum, now they found themselves in a political vacuum. There are multi-party systems, but parties seem very similar to each other. The only well-organised one is the 'transformed' or really transformed communist party, as seen in all of the countries in question during their first free elections. People might have voted against the communists, but they voted for those most similar to them. They opted for the familiar. Having lived so long under communism and having no solid democratic tradition, they could not develop an interest in politics overnight, or participate actively in the complicated political life of the new period. To be involved in politics was always to be an opportunist, aiming to get a better job, to promote a career or to get better pay. Under communism politics was something distant and dangerous, something to fear and hate, certainly not something to get involved in.

After all, the two most terrible dictators in Eastern Europe were Nicolae Ceauşescu in Romania and Enver Hoxha in Albania. Communism breeds only masses, not individuals, not citizens. Citizens who are aware of their rights and able to fight for them are only found in a democracy. In the communist mass society very few people believed that a single individual could bring about change. In Romania, during two consecutive free elections, the crypto-communists were voted into office (the same thing happened in Serbia). The Romanians overwhelmingly (85 per cent of them) supported Ion Iliescu for president in preference to some competent but grey bureaucrat who would work on behalf of democracy. It is wrong to assume that they did it because they did not know what they were doing. On the contrary, they did know, and they did it because they felt they needed such a party and such a personality. They saw in Iliescu a strong character, a strong leader who would guide them through rough transitory times. People did not want a dramatic break, even if that would have released them from their prison; they needed a feeling of continuity.

Romanians and Serbs alike reached for familiar solutions in similar situations: a known party; a strong leader. In turbulent times, times of dramatic social and political change, people tend to fall back on what they know. Before, the only identification one was allowed was with the working class, yet, underneath that lid there was one's own nationality, language, religion and culture to identify with. Nationality and religion became props, sticks people could not walk without, something known and secure to give them the new identity they needed. The immediate rise of nationalism and religious feeling right after the fall of communism, and to a dangerous degree (as happened in former Yugoslavia and the former USSR) speaks for itself. What else was there to identify with? The new political game and its leaders had only just started to emerge, and were unknown and mistrusted; there were no democratic traditions to facilitate the transformation of society and no

civic institutions one could count on. As Ryszard Kapus-
ćiński writes in his book *Imperium*, the concept of *perestroika* came from 'above'. In other words, the idea of
democratisation did not come from 'below', from the
people themselves. They were too frightened to dare to
demand anything like democracy. Like everything else, it
was initiated from the very top.

After the break with the communist past, there was a
desperate almost palpable need to establish a firm link with
the pre-war or pre-communist past. Thus Slovakia or
Croatia, two newly independent states, quickly established
links with the only period of 'independence' of which they
had a collective memory – unfortunately the fascist period
under Josef Tiso and Ante Pavelić respectively. These two
new states did not have any past monarchies to relate to.
Poland, the Czech Republic and Hungary had at least some
democratic traditions to claim as their heritage. On the
other hand, kings of the Balkan countries were there, at
hand, as living proof of the past. What could be more
logical than to try to bring them back to their respective
countries in order to restore the monarchies there? Well, in
my view, it would merely replace one kind of feudalism
with another.

If you take a closer look at Balkan communist leaders like
Nicolae Ceauşescu, Enver Hoxha, Josip Broz Tito or Todor
Zhivkov, a clear feudal pattern to their rule can be
discerned. They treated their citizens as mere objects of
their political or other whims; they wielded almost absolute
power over people's lives; they lived in palaces, some
confiscated from former kings (like Beli Dvor in Belgrade),
others, even bigger, were built by the dictators themselves
(Ceauşescu); they established their relatives in key positions
and rewarded their faithful vassals; they had courts of

servants at their disposal, as well as their own army and police; they were only formally responsible to their parliaments or to the communist party. In these Balkan countries, communism was in a way a continuity of feudalism. Therefore, the desire to re-establish the monarchy in these Balkan countries is not an archaic, outdated idea in modern Europe, but one that has never died, and which would guarantee continuity with the past, perhaps even a certain political stability.

One needs to understand that we, the people from the communist world, are still children in the political sense. We need a daddy, somebody who will look after us, so that we don't have to look after ourselves. We don't know how to be free and we are not ready for responsibility. The result is a palpable disappointment with the new, post-communist reality. How come democracy doesn't work? Democracy does not work just because our presidents say it does, or because we have a new, democratic constitution, a multi-party system, free elections, a free-market economy. These are only basic preconditions for building democracy; it is us, all of us, who have to make it work. To know how to do it, we need to learn from those who have some experience. But who likes to go to school? Not us.

Perhaps an enlightened monarchy is not such a bad solution after all. If people feel the need for a father figure, they are going to install him one way or another, so wouldn't it be better to have a ready-made historical figure, such as a king, rather than yet another shoeless maverick who will turn into both a king and a dictator as soon as he grabs power? A nice, educated rich king, who would fulfil that paternal role for an adolescent nation and, at the same time, would feel a noble duty to serve his people, would not necessarily be an obstacle to the development of democracy. Look at England, the Netherlands or Sweden. On the contrary, a monarch would perhaps help people to adjust to a new political and economic reality, devoting time to the construction of the institutions of a civic society, the development of private ownership and a proper middle class with liberal values: in short, the essence of any functioning democracy. And if this sounds anachronistic, isn't the whole idea of establishing ethnically clean nation states, which is nourished in the Balkans today, equally anachronistic – and more costly in terms of peace and human lives?

If a king is the answer to many of the fears and anxieties of the masses in the Balkan countries, then long live the king! Perhaps, having helped the country to its feet, he would confine himself to the symbolic representation of the state, leaving politics to more competent people while he takes time off to go sailing, like the Swedish King. Such a figure is the opposite of what we have in Croatia today: an absolutist, theatrical king without a crown or sceptre, but with all attributes of the royalty; and of Slobodan Milošević in Serbia, a dictator who is willing to pay any price to stay in power. Leaders like him are too greedy for power and have no chance to learn the very first lesson of democracy: that they are there to serve their people, not to rule them. And if that is so, wouldn't it be better for Serbs to have a real king, His Royal Highness Crown Prince Alexander Karadjordjević? Perhaps Croatia could produce someone, too?

Buying a Vacuum Cleaner

The other day my husband had one of his terrible choleric attacks. That morning, sipping his coffee, he was already irritable. I knew the reason only too well. The next day we were supposed to go to our summer house in Croatia for a holiday. To get there, from Vienna, we obviously have to cross the Croatian state border. The mere thought of that is enough to set him off.

The last time we crossed that border, leaving Croatia, he had one of these attacks. A customs officer stopped us and asked if we had anything to declare. What do you want us to declare, what is there to take out of Croatia?, my husband started to shout, red in the face – in English, thank God, so the customs officer did not understand. My husband was so upset by this unnecessary pestering that he did not even stop to show the police officer our passports, but just drove on. The policeman was shouting after us, and I demanded that we return to the sentry box. We pass through that particular crossing, only 6 kilometres from our house, at least once a month, if not more going to Trieste for shopping. I did not want to give the officers there a reason to remember us and to take their revenge and complicate our lives by really pestering us every time we cross the border. The young policeman, who was by now red in the face as well, warned us politely that we should have stopped, because rules are rules. I humbly apologised, showed our passports and we drove on. Now my husband's face was getting pale, he was shaking and he did not want to drive any longer. He accused me of being an accomplice of the system of humiliation at the border.

Of course, I immediately recognised one of his classical attacks of border phobia, which manifest themselves first in irritation – which can start a couple of days in advance – then in extreme excitement, next in aggression, and finally in a kind of depression for the rest of the day. My husband is actually the nicest, most peaceful man in the whole universe, but the problem is that he is still a foreigner in this part of the world. It might be better if he was a complete foreigner, but he is a Swede married to a Croat. This border phobia is, I believe, also a long-term legacy of his job. As a newspaper correspondent in Eastern Europe of more than twenty years' standing, he has been exposed to all kinds of harassment and he simply can't stand it any longer. 'For half of my life, upon entering Eastern Europe, I have been treated like a criminal, a spy or something even worse,' he used to say. Crossing borders into Czechoslovakia, Bulgaria or Romania in the seventies and eighties, cannot have been much fun for the correspondent of a Western paper. One needs only to think of the visas, car searches and sometimes even body searches to imagine the humiliation he used to feel. It became an emotional issue to him, and he cannot always rationally handle such situations.

What makes him angry now is that the situation at the border after the fall of communism is even worse, at least in Croatia. This new state has to prove to itself that it is a real independent state on every level, which seems to have to involve being arrogant to everyone going in or out of it. Every car entering the country by road is checked. Croatian citizens may bring in only $100 worth of goods, the same limit that applied to former Yugoslavia. And if you disregard this rule and are caught, you have to pay over 30 per cent in duty. A very unpleasant attitude on the part of customs and police officers is included in the package. For people travelling by air, customs have now installed a scanner at Zagreb Airport. Your luggage is not only screened when you leave the country, as it is at every airport in the world, but also upon your arrival from abroad, so that the quota of $100 per citizen can be properly checked. All luggage must pass the screening machine – there is no green 'nothing to declare' zone. There is a sign indicating one, but if you try to follow it, you will encounter only locked doors.

'Why don't you, citizens of the new democratic Croatia, do something about it?' says my husband.

'Like what?' I ask.

'Like protesting, demanding a change of these absurd rules. Why don't you even remonstrate with those rude customs officers?' What he means is why are we still obeying the authorities as we did before, under communism?

Well, why don't we do something? But we do, of course we do. We fight the system using the subtle method we have used for forty-five years: subversion. It is a completely rational method; one could call it a survivalist form of behaviour. Before, it was impossible to beat the communist system in any other way but subversion. You had to obey or you would end up in jail. You knew that the authorities would always be able to find something wrong with your passport (if you had one), with the money you were taking out of the country (if you had it), with documents, with just about anything. You were in the wrong on principle, a subject who had to be regularly humiliated in order to be put in your place.

What is a normal, healthy reaction to this? It is, of course, to steal a march on the officials by cheating. This is the logic of it: the humiliation to which you are subjected (suspicion, arrogance, checking, restrictions, being made to pay) you look upon as a part of the police or customs officer's job, and you get used to it. It is not nice, but you can't afford to raise your voice, to quarrel with them or to rebel. Experience tells you that this path leads nowhere at best and might end badly for you. To cheat the system is part of the same game, the other side of the coin. The system forces you into smuggling (if you can call bringing home goods worth slightly more than $100 *smuggling*), and the officers at the border understand this very well.

This criminalisation of the entire population, turning everybody into a petty criminal, serves as a kind of control. You smuggle, therefore you are not only a suspect (in fact an innocent victim of the arrogance of the state) but automatically a petty criminal in any case. So, you say nothing: you obey, you pay if they catch you, and you count on the law of averages – it is physically impossible for them to catch everybody. You buy what you can and take your chances. If they stop you, start searching and find, say, a cellular telephone or a fax machine, you simply pay the duty without protest. It is still worth it, because even with the duty, you pay less for such goods than you would in your country.

Looking at it from my husband's point of view, this

whole attitude, that of the customs officers as well as that of the people, is simply unacceptable, especially today, when borders between countries of the European Union virtually no longer exist. 'So what if people go and buy where it's cheaper?' he says. 'They have the right to do so.' Of course, he is right. The local currency, the kuna, is 40 per cent overvalued, according to the International Monetary Fund, and is not even convertible. Food prices are on average 30 to 100 per cent higher than in Austria, one of the most expensive countries in Western Europe. So people just cross the border, buy cheaper food and electrical goods, and take the risk of being caught with them.

In that respect, nothing has changed since the communist times. But obviously such traffic poses a problem for our already devastated national economy (hundreds of thousands, perhaps even millions, of German marks are spent abroad each month), so much so that one representative of the Croatian parliament proposed the abolition of even the paltry $100 limit, forbidding citizens to bring anything at all into the country. This story ended with a ridiculous appeal to the Croatian citizens: be a patriot, buy Croatian products! Fine, but who can afford them? So, the method of survival by regular smuggling goes on.

Buying a vacuum cleaner in such conditions is not an easy task. I know it is hard to believe that a simple vacuum cleaner could be a problem, but it can. If you have one, and it breaks down, you are faced with two options: you either have it repaired or you buy a new one. In Croatia today, both of these solutions are equally painful, at least they were in my case. To repair my vacuum cleaner was difficult, because the factory that produced it was now in another country: Slovenia. It would be hard to get spare parts: you have to order them, wait a long time and pay a lot, too, because they would be treated as an import. My vacuum cleaner was so old that it was beyond repair anyway, so I decided I would have to buy a new one. After some market research, my husband and I discovered that, like most things in Croatia, vacuum cleaners were 30 to 50 per cent more expensive than they were in Austria, either because they were imported, or overpriced, or both.

The only logical solution was to buy one abroad. But, because of the $100 limit, we had to do a bit of planning – there are not many vacuum cleaners you could buy for less than that sum. The usual way to go about this is to get a fake bill from the shop where you buy your goods. This is not a problem in Italy, especially in Trieste or in any of the shops close to the Italian border. The shop will issue you a receipt for, say, $99, even though you have paid them $250. The customs officers do not usually object, even if they suspect that your bill is a fake, unless the manipulation is much too obvious and the price ridiculously low (this teaches you that your cheating has to be plausible!). They don't object because they don't have a quick way of verifying prices, they can only estimate them, because the piece of paper is all they need to cover themselves.

However, as we live in Vienna for part of the year, we decided to buy a vacuum cleaner there. But when we inquired in several shops about a fake bill, we discovered that the Austrians, apparently, have never heard of such a trick. In one big shop they looked at us as if we were criminals; I even had the feeling that they might call the police as soon as we turned our backs and walked out of the shop. This was strange, because we were in Maria Hilfer Street, the main shopping area for Eastern Europeans. You can hardly hear the German language there, and everyone knows that every Romanian, Hungarian, Croat or Slovak has to smuggle things or pay customs.

In the end, we found a small, privately owned shop, because we figured that it would be less bureaucratic, and that the owner might want to help us if we explained to him why we needed such a receipt. The man showed some understanding and was prepared to do us a favour, but at the crucial point, my husband made a mistake. He remarked that the vacuum cleaner we intended to buy was about 10 per cent cheaper in other shops in the vicinity. 'Then go and buy it there! I don't want to sell you anything now!' the man exclaimed, offended. My husband suffered only a minor choleric attack, explaining to the man in a very polite manner, though in a highly irritated tone, that if he went on treating his customers in this way, he'd soon go bankrupt. This only made the shopkeeper more angry, and he literally threw us out of his shop.

Tired of this useless search and risking my husband's fury, I dared to suggest that we simply bought a vacuum cleaner and got a normal bill. If we were caught with it we'd pay duty, but so what? He stubbornly stuck to his principles of not overtly smuggling. 'Money was not the issue,' he said. This is where I got mad: surely the point of this whole exercise was to save money? 'No, the point is that it is stupid to pay customs!' he said.

'Then let's buy the bloody thing in Croatia and at least save ourselves all this trouble.'

'But it is even more stupid to pay 50 per cent extra there for a vacuum cleaner,' he insisted.

'If we pay the duty, we still would be saving money,' I retorted.

'Don't you see that this is part of the same idiocy?' he said, really angry now.

Using my last argument, I said: 'But we need a vacuum

cleaner, and we *can* afford to buy one in Croatia, or to pay duty if we buy it here.'

This he could not contest, but as we had two radically opposite viewpoints, we decided to drop the subject for a while.

When he went away for a couple of days I decided to take this problem into my own hands, because I needed to go to Zagreb anyway, so I would buy the damned vacuum cleaner behind his back and take it back with me on the train. He would not even know about my little diversion, and what you don't know can't hurt you. A nice plan, indeed, but it did not work. I had to postpone my train journey and the brand new Rowenta vacuum cleaner that I found in a sale for an amazing $99 had to wait in the apartment in Vienna, packed in an innocent-looking travelling bag. In the meantime, my husband returned from his business trip and we started to pack for Zagreb. I reminded him that we needed to buy a special liquid to protect the walls of our house in Croatia against humidity. He wanted to know if it would be within the $100 limit (as a foreigner, he has no right to bring in anything at all except his personal belongings). Then I had to admit to my little plan concerning the Rowenta. Now that I had bought it, it somehow has to be transported to Croatia, I said. 'OK, but we'll have to leave the liquid behind,' he said. I tried to persuade him that we needed that too, but it was useless. I saw his face getting red, and I stopped myself right there. An extremely nice, rational and controlled man of fifty was about to freak out again, all because of a stupid vacuum cleaner. I wanted to spare him that.

I understand his irritation completely. When he calms down, he understands my cool, calculated, shrewd persona as a 'professional' Eastern European smuggler. What he cannot understand is why 'we' (and here I instantly become 'one of them'), the citizens of the newly liberated countries, stand it at all.

I don't understand it myself. I could give him a hundred reasons why 'we' do not fight for principles – the war, poor economy, fear, lack of a proper democracy – but they would probably all boil down to the fact that we are still busy fighting for our survival, perhaps even harder than before. Furthermore, we do not really believe that change is possible. Perhaps it is because things are not changing quickly enough. We still have a one-party government, corruption, injustice, poverty and ladder-climbing, very much as we did before. But when I look at my own words, that passive 'are not changing', I see where it all begins, I understand the trap: those words imply that somebody else has to do it for us. Even I, in my own head, have not made the definite step from 'them' to 'me', from communism to democracy.

I don't know what the solution is. All I know is that I cannot wait at the border with my new vacuum cleaner until my country becomes a member of the European Union or a real democratic country.

In the end, my husband allowed me to take my precious Rowenta in the car – but nothing else, of course. At the Croatian border near Zagreb, a customs officer asked his usual question: 'Do you have anything to declare?' No, I say, as always. I am not even lying, not this time, because my Rowenta cost less than $100. But I would have said no even if it had cost $1,000, simply because I don't think that I could have brought myself to say that yes, indeed, I did have something to declare. Not in the near future, anyway.

A Nostalgic Party at the Graveyard

In Bucharest, 26 January 1994 was an extraordinarily cold day. It was bright and sunny, but
the temperature was perhaps minus 10 degrees
Celsius, and as soon as you got out in the street, you would
instantly stop feeling your fingers, toes, ears and the tip of
your nose. It was certainly not a day to visit the graveyard,
unless you absolutely had to. It was a midweek working day,
but oddly there was a mass of people heading towards the
Ghencea Cemetery. The funeral of someone important
perhaps? No, that was not it: something much more bizarre
was going on there.

As I soon discovered, the people were on their way to
visit the grave of the executed dictator Nicolae Ceauşescu.
This would have been his seventy-fifth birthday. And had
he been alive, what a celebration it would have been! A
national holiday, no less, with hundreds of flags fluttering,
Ceauşescu's picture exhibited in every shop window,
decorated with red carnations, and, of course, a special
television broadcast in which he would address the nation.
The biggest event would have taken place in the main

football stadium, packed to the rafters, where young people would have performed a carefully choreographed kind of mass 'ballet' for the Greatest Son of Romania; grey-haired academicians would have made speeches about his extraordinary historical merits; poets would have recited their poems glorifying him and kindergarten children would have sung appropriate songs. I knew exactly how it would have looked – I have seen such celebrations so many times on Tito's birthday in Yugoslavia.

But Ceauşescu was dead, executed. His grave was a simple mound without a tombstone (supposedly it disappeared) decorated with a lot of fresh and paper carnations, flickering candles and red Communist Party flags. There were also gifts of bread and cakes, in the Orthodox tradition, and on top of all that, his photograph. There was Ceauşescu, in all his glory, his retouched rosy cheeks glowing, his retouched blue eyes beaming and his non-retouched self-assured dictator's smile still in place, as if nothing could happen to him – ever.

At ten o'clock on that chilly morning, Ceauşescu's grave was surrounded by about 150 people. They murmured, a few women cried openly, there were exclamations and a slight feeling of growing tension, as if they were expecting something to happen, someone to come and address them. At first I was confused. Who were they, and why were they showing up to pay tribute to a dictator at a time when in other countries people were celebrating their deliverance from their communist past, even to the extent that they were attempting to annihilate it completely?

I could not decide if this strange gathering was a birthday party or a political demonstration. As I mused on this, they started to sing and call out slogans. 'Unite, workers, unite! Say no to the capitalist slavery!' they sang, as if they really believed in these words. Then an old but vigorous man shouted: 'Why were you murdered?', while people around him recited like a Greek chorus, 'Americans and Russians are to blame for our poverty?' Indeed, for a moment I felt as if I were present at the staging of a soc-realist drama about the proletariate, as if these people were actors, not real people. A woman wrapped in a black woollen shawl came out, in front of the chorus. 'Before, we used to send our children to summer camps!' she exclaimed, waving her fist in the air towards the invisible enemies who had taken away summer camps from her children, as if she would take her revenge at any moment. Then another woman took her place. 'With my pension, I can buy one kilo of meat a month,' she said. It was expressed like a prepared statement, in a matter-of-fact voice without anger, but perhaps with sadness. Her performance got strong support from the chorus, who sang, 'Yes, yes,' to echo her words.

Indeed, this was an improvised political drama, unfolding around Ceauşescu's grave, with members of the public coming out to tell their personal troubles, more to each other than to Ceauşescu himself. It took me a while, but eventually I understood that they had not so much come there to freeze in celebration of his birthday, or even merely to pay tribute to Ceauşescu as their beloved leader. They had come together to remember their own better past. They were mostly elderly people: they looked like retired workers, old soldiers, peasants, old Communist Party apparatchiks; people who perhaps had profited from the previous regime and for whom the change had come too late. They looked poor and lost in their thin, worn-out coats, rubber boots and fur hats. At least, they had had more to eat before; at least their children had had proper holidays before.

The only period with which they could identify was the

communist era. Perhaps they did not cry for Ceauşescu himself; perhaps he was merely the symbol of all they knew and remembered. Among the crowd, I spotted Ceauşescu's brother Flora, the former minister of agriculture – the dictator's nepotism was well known. It was easy to spot him, because of his marked resemblance to Nicolae. By looking at Flora, you could get a realistic, not retouched, picture of the old Nicolae. I asked him how he interpreted this gathering at the graveyard. Was it a celebration? Some kind of demonstration? He gave me a simplistic Marxist explanation, but you would expect nothing less from a member of the Ceauşescu clan. 'If the economy were better, there would be no need to revive him. But the worse it gets, the more people will want to revive my brother.' True, the fall of communism had brought only misery to the people at the graveyard, and to many more besides. All their lives they had worked a little, earned barely enough money to survive, but they had felt safe. They were educated to believe that the Ceauşescu regime would be eternal; they collaborated with the regime and gained their small privileges from that; they cheated and stole state property. Each of them was a part of an obedient and fear-struck mass in a country that was a kind of penal colony.

And then it was all over. The change was totally unpredicted, totally abrupt. They are not able to cope with it and their entire generation, the people over fifty, never will be. They will remain bitter and unhappy; they will not understand anything about politics, much less about democracy. These people, who would prefer Ceauşescu to be alive, who would prefer the old regime because they knew how to cope with it, how to deal with it day by day, even if the price for that was slavery, are the real losers today. The single word that sums up their lives is 'complicity'. There are many of them, too many to enable this country to move forward quickly. There, at Ceauşescu's grave, I felt sorry for them. How terrible it must be to have no place of pilgrimage other than Ceauşescu's grave.

I have heard it said that Nicolae and his wife Elena were not buried together. Someone explained to me that no one knows exactly where she is buried, because the corpses were brought to the graveyard in the middle of the night. It was a very secret operation. Perhaps later on both of them were even dug up and put somewhere else to rest, so that people would not gather at their graves, either to take their revenge or out of nostalgia. No one could confirm that Nicolae Ceauşescu really was buried in the grave bearing his name, but apparently, even the possibility that he lies there was enough to bring people to it that day.

The case of Elena's grave is a different matter. When I asked if someone knew where her grave was, there was a moment of commotion. Then, to my surprise, one man pointed, with great authority, to a nameless mound about 15 metres away. I went over and stood there for a while, wondering whether it really was her grave and how the man had known that for certain. The only possible answer was that he knew because he was a policeman. But if so, then, why would he have told me where it was? Was it a kind of secret, or did people just not pay any attention to the grave of Ceauşescu's wife? Elena was, to say the least, not very popular.

The grave was surrounded by an iron fence and had no sign, name, cross, flower – nothing. Just yellow frozen clay, like a mudcake, to seal it. No, the Romanians did not like Elena. To them, she was quintessentially evil, a witch, the mean, driving power behind her husband, a real dictator with blood on her hands. There are innumerable anecdotes about her cruelty and cynical behaviour, and stories about spying on her own children, especially her daughter Zoe (apparently, the mother ordered a camera to be installed in her bedroom). As well as being a dictator's wife and the second most powerful person in the country, Elena was also an aspiring 'scientist' specialising in chemistry, with dozens of self-awarded titles, honours and medals. Immediately after she was executed along with her husband, the Romanian newspapers were full of articles mocking her 'achievements', for example, her method of curing flu with boiling water. In order to prove that her cure worked, she is said to have gone to an orphanage, picked up a sick baby and dipped it into boiling water. Of course, the flu was cured but the patient didn't survive the treatment. This could hardly be a true story, but it reflects the image of Elena people had. Not only was she terribly cruel, but she was powerful beyond any kind of responsibility, a real master of life and death. No wonder, then, that with such an opinion of her, Romanians couldn't care less where she was buried.

But while I was standing at the graveside a strange thing happened. A stocky man in blue overalls appeared out of what appeared to be the mortuary. He carried a big, newly made wooden cross. He took it to the grave which had been identified to me as Elena's and started to dig a hole for it, at the same time delivering a kind of speech. It was not easy to dig because the ground was frozen and hard, and the man had to work hard to make a hole, but it did not interrupt his monologue. Aware that something was going on, the people at Nicolae Ceauşescu's graveside came over and gathered around. Soon there was a crowd at this officially anonymous grave. The man in the blue overalls continued to dig slowly, and in long, disconnected sentences mused about poverty, *nomenklatura*, power. He was digging deep now, and it occurred to me that he was not afraid of suddenly hitting the coffin. Even if his speech did not make much sense, people stood there, this time in silence, as if bewitched by the rhythmic movements of his hands and the dull thud of the shovel hitting the ground. It looked as if he was trying to dig something out, a long-forgotten ghost that might emerge from the hole at any moment.

The people around me were obviously intrigued by the fact that, in front of their own eyes, Elena's grave was finally to be given some kind of symbol, a sign that she had existed, a cross. A woman standing next to me asked if I had a pen. I handed it to her and she bravely walked up to the cross and started to write Elena's name on it. She misspelled it, poor soul, and had to correct her mistake, and by the time she had finished, the inscription looked messy and awkward, as if it had been written by a barely literate person. But it was there, at least. In the meantime, the gravedigger's voice grew louder and louder, his face red with exaltation. Someone told me that he was drunk. Finally, he succeeded in putting up the cross. A murmur of excitement stirred the people like a breath of wind. A few women approached the cross and put flowers under it. I could not shake off the suspicion that they had taken them from a fresh grave nearby.

The whole scene was pathetic and moving at the same time. There they were, ordinary Romanians, giving a name to the anonymous grave of Elena Ceauşescu, the name that had been denied her by the new men in power. Even if she was the hated wife of a dictator, she still was a human being and therefore she deserved a grave with her name on it.

The midday sun was pale and cold, but no one seemed to mind that as they stood there in silence. Then, slowly, the people left.

I could not help wondering how it could happen that the cross for Elena's grave should arrive on that very day, at that very moment. If it was really meant for her, why was her name not already written on it? I did not expect answers to these questions. But when the party at the graveside was over, a local reporter (or so he introduced himself to me) told me that it was not Elena's grave, and the cross was not meant for her, but for someone else who was to be buried later that afternoon. The whole impromptu restoration of her name had been created by a single, drunken gravedigger. Whatever the truth, that theatrical performance somehow fitted into my picture of Romania today.

On Bad Teeth

In a way, I was initiated into capitalism through toothpaste.

When I first visited the States in 1983, I loved to watch TV commercials. This is when I noticed that Americans were obsessed by their teeth. Every second commercial seemed to be for a toothpaste. Where I come from, toothpaste is toothpaste. I couldn't believe there were so many different kinds. What were they all *for*? After all, the purpose of it is just to clean your teeth. In my childhood there were two kinds, mint flavour and strawberry flavour, and both of them had the same brand name, Kalodont. For a long time I was convinced that Kalodont was the word for toothpaste, because nobody at home used the generic word. We never said, 'Do you have toothpaste?', we said, 'Do you have Kalodont?' It is hardly surprising, then, that such a person would react with nothing short of disbelief when faced with the American cosmetic (or is it pharmaceutical?) industry and its endless production line. Toothpaste with or without sugar, with or without flour, with or without baking soda, calcium, vitamins . . .

Over the years, on subsequent visits I continued to be fascinated by this American obsession with toothpaste, from the common varieties all the way up to Rembrandt, the most snobbish brand, if there could be such a thing as snobbishness about toothpaste. I soon learned that there could: in one women's magazine I saw it recommended as a Christmas present! Needless to say, in every commercial for toothpaste at least one bright, impressively beautiful set of teeth flashes across the screen, but this image is not confined to selling toothpaste. As we all know, beautiful teeth are used to advertise beer, hair shampoo, cars, anything. Indeed, they are an indispensable feature of any American advertisement. The foreigner soon learns that they stand not only as a symbol for both good looks and good health, but for something else as well.

If you think that such advertising might be part of the Americans' national obsession with health in general, you are not far from the truth. Americans seem to be passionate about their health and their looks, which appear to be interchangeable qualities. Health and good looks are essential badges of status among the middle classes. Nothing but narcissism, you could retort, but it is more than that. This connection between teeth and social status is not so evident to an Eastern European. I personally had some doubts about those TV teeth, I thought that they must be artificial, some kind of prosthesis made out of plastic or porcelain. They were just too good to be true. How could people have such fine teeth? Intrigued, I decided to take a good look around me.

I noticed that the people I met, that is mostly middle-class urban professionals, generally do have a set of bright, white teeth of their own, not unlike the TV teeth. It was even more surprising to me that I could detect no cavities, no missing teeth, no imperfections. I was astonished. The secret was revealed to me when a friend took her son to the dentist. When they returned, the little boy's upper teeth were fixed with a dreadful-looking kind of iron muzzle: a brace, I learned. It was obviously painful for him. 'Poor little thing!' I exclaimed, but his mother showed no mercy. Moreover, she was proud that she could afford this torture device. I was puzzled. When she explained to me that the brace cost between $2,000 and $3,000, her attitude seemed even more sinister. I eventually realised that the mystery of beautiful teeth is not only about hygiene, but about money. She had money enough to get her son's teeth fixed, and the little boy was brave enough to stand the pain, because somehow he understood that this was a requirement of his social status. All the other boys from his private school had braces, too. He was going to grow up being well aware of the fact that his healthy, beautiful teeth were expensive and, therefore, an indication of prestige. Moreover, his mother could count on him to brush them three times a day, with an electric toothbrush and the latest toothpaste promising even healthier and more beautiful teeth, as if that were possible. In the long run, all the discomfort would be worth it.

Seeing the boy's brace, the connection between health and wealth in America became a bit clearer to me. Clean, healthy teeth feature so much in advertising because Americans have no free dental care, and neither is it covered by any medical insurance. Therefore, if you invest money and educate your child early enough (a bit of suffering is needed, too), you will save a lot later. But how much money did this take? I got my answer when I had to visit a dentist myself. On one of my last visits my filling fell out, and just to have it refilled with some temporary white stuff, whatever it was, I had to pay $100. This would be a minor financial catastrophe for any Eastern European citizen used to free dental care in his own country; it was expensive even by American standards. Only then did I become fully aware of what it means not to have free dental care.

Predictably enough, I was outraged. How was it possible for dental work to be so expensive in this country? For $100 back home I could have coated my tooth in pure gold! And why was it that such an affluent country did not provide its citizens with basic services like free dental work? This was one of the very few areas in which we from former communist countries had some advantage over Americans – and we would like to keep it.

On my way home, I thought what a blessing it was that we did not have to worry about our teeth, or about whether we could afford to look after them – or at least, we did not have to worry yet, in my country, anyway. However, immediately upon my arrival in Zagreb, I realised that I could allow myself such rose-tinted thoughts only as long as I was on the other side of the Atlantic, from where everything at home looked a bit blurred, especially the general state of people's teeth. Back at home, I was forced to adjust my view. It was as if I had been myopic before and now I had got the right pair of glasses and could finally see properly. And what I saw did not please me at all.

On the bus from the airport I met one of my acquaintances, a young television reporter. For the first time I noticed that half of his teeth were missing and that those which remained looked like the ruins of a decayed medieval town. I had known this guy for years, but I had never thought about the state of the inside of his mouth before, or if I had, I'd considered it totally unimportant. Now I also noticed that, in order to hide his bad teeth, he had grown a moustache and developed a way of laughing which didn't involve him opening his mouth too wide. Even so, his bad teeth were still obvious.

This encounter did not cheer me up. Sitting next to the young reporter, I wondered how he managed to speak in front of a TV camera without making a mistake that would reveal his terrible secret. Without smiling, perhaps? This would be perfectly acceptable, because he reports on the war, but wasn't he tired of this uncomfortable game of hide-and-seek? Wouldn't it be much more professional and make life easier if he visited a good dentist and got it all over with? But this is not something we are supposed to talk about. How do you say such a thing to a person if he is not your intimate friend? You can't just say, 'Listen, why don't you do something about your teeth?' Perhaps I should have pulled out my toothpaste and handed it to him, or casually dropped the name of my dentist, something like what my friend did last summer. A woman standing next to her in a streetcar emanated an extremely unpleasant odour from her hairy armpits. My friend could not stand it. She pulled her own deodorant stick out of her handbag and gave it to the woman. The funny thing is that the woman accepted it without taking offence. I, on the other hand, could not risk offending my acquaintance.

I continued my investigations at home. Yes, I admit that I looked into the mouths of friends, relatives, acquaintances, neighbours – I could not help it. I discovered that the whole nation had bad teeth, it was just that I had not been able to see it before. I concluded that the guy on the bus was only a part of the general landscape, that he was no exception, and that therefore his failure to attend to his teeth was perfectly normal. I tried to explain this attitude to myself: perhaps people were afraid of drilling? Of course. Who isn't? But if nothing else, there must be an aesthetic drive in every human being, or one would at least think so. Yet, for some reason, aesthetics and communism don't go well together and though we might call our current state post-communism, we still have a communist attitude in such matters.

You could also argue that dentists, being employed by the state, are not well paid. Consequently, they don't put much effort into their job. You can claim as well that the materials they use are not of good quality. That is all probably true. But, I still believe that having your teeth repaired to a mediocre standard is preferable to treasuring the medieval ruins in your mouth or being toothless altogether.

There is no excuse that sounds reasonable enough for such negligence. The problem is that the condition of your teeth in Eastern Europe is regarded as a highly personal matter, not a sign of your standard of living or a question for public discussion. Having good teeth is simply a matter of being civilised and well mannered. Strangely enough, however, dirty shoes, dirty fingernails or dandruff are no longer tolerated: these are considered impolite, even offensive. Yet like such matters of personal hygiene, good teeth are not only a question of money. Dental work has been free for the last forty years. At present there co-exists a mixture of both state-run general medical care, which includes dental care, and private dentists. If you want, you can have excellent dental work done. I know people who travel from Vienna to Bratislava, Budapest, Ljubljana or Zagreb to have their teeth repaired more cheaply. But if you asked people in Eastern Europe who can afford it why they don't go to a private dentist for a better service, they would probably tell you that this is not their priority at the moment. Instead they want to fix their car, or buy a new carpet.

It is clear that leaders and intellectuals here certainly don't care about such a minor aspect of their image. They are preoccupied with the destiny of their respective nations, they do not have time for such trivial matters. The American idea that it is not very polite for a public figure to appear with bad teeth, just as it would be inappropriate to make a speech in your pyjamas, is not understood here. You can meet exquisitely dressed politicians or business-men, but wait until they open their mouths! If these public figures are not worried about this aspect of their looks, why should ordinary people be concerned about theirs? They too have more important things to do, for example surviving. There is also that new breed, the *nouveau riche* of post-communism. Previously everything was valued by one's participation in politics, now it is slowly replaced by money. The arrogance of these people originates there. Unfortunately, money does not guarantee good manners, or a regular visit to the dentist for that matter.

I can only try to imagine the horrors when free dental work is replaced by private dentists whose prices nobody can afford. How many decades will we have to wait until our teeth look like American ones? It is a question of perception. In order to improve your looks, you have to be convinced that it is worth the trouble. In other words, we are dealing with a problem of self-esteem, with a way of thinking, rather than a superficial question. Bad teeth are the result of bad dentists and bad food, but also of a specific culture of thinking, of not seeing yourself as an individual. What we need here is a revolution of self-perception. Not only will that not come automatically with the new political changes, but I am afraid that it will also take longer than any political or economic developments. We need to accept our responsibilities towards both others and ourselves. This is not only a wise sort of investment in the future, as we can see in the case of Americans, it also gives you the feeling that you have done what you can to improve yourself, be it your teeth, your health, your career, education, environment or society in general.

Individual responsibility, including the responsibility for oneself, in an entirely new concept here, as I have stated many times elsewhere. This is why the revolution of self-perception has a long way to go. As absurd as it may sound, in the old days one could blame the Communist Party even for one's bad teeth. Now there is no one to blame, but it takes time to understand that. If you have never had it, self-respect has to be learned. Maybe our own teeth would be a good place to start.

But I can see signs of coming changes. Recently a good friend borrowed some money from me in order to repair her apartment. When the time came to give it back, she told me that I would have to wait, because she needed the money for something very urgent. She had finally decided to have her teeth fixed by a private dentist. No wonder she was left without a penny. But what could I have said to that? I said the only thing I could say: 'I understand you, this must come first.'

Finally, I guess it is only fair that I should declare the state of my own teeth. I am one of those who much too often used the free dental work so generously provided by the communist state for the benefit of its people. I was afraid of the dentist, all right, but also brave enough to stand the pain because I had overcome the psychological barrier at an early age.

When I was in the third grade a teacher showed us a cartoon depicting a fortress – a tooth – attacked by bad guys – bacteria. They looked terribly dangerous, digging tunnels and ditches with their small axes until the fortress almost fell into their hands. Then the army of good guys, the white blood cells, arrived and saved it at the last moment. The teacher explained to us how we could fight the bad guys by brushing our teeth regularly with Kalodont and by visiting a dentist every time we spotted a little hole or felt pain. I took her advice literally – I was obviously very impressed by the cartoon, just as I was impressed by the American TV commercials thirty years later. The result is that today I can say that I have good teeth, although six of them are missing. How did that happen? Well, when I spotted a little cavity, I would immediately go to the dentist all by myself. This was mistake number one. You could not choose your own dentist at that time, and my family had to go to a military hospital. A dentist there would usually fill the cavity, but for some reason the filling would soon fall out. Then he would make an even bigger hole and fill it again, until eventually there was not much tooth left.

Those 'dentists' were in fact young students of dentistry drafted into the army. For them, this was probably an excellent chance to improve their knowledge by practising on patients. When they'd finished practising on me a more experienced dentist would suggest I had the tooth out. What could I, a child, do but agree? This was mistake number two, of course. I had to learn to live with one gap in my jaw, then another, and another. Much later I had two bridges made by a private dentist. He didn't even ask me why I was missing six of my teeth; he knew how things had worked in those days. My only consolation was that I did not have to pay much for my bridgework.

Like everyone else in the post-communist world, I had to learn the meaning of the American proverb 'There is no such thing as a free lunch.' The Americans are right. You don't get anything properly done if you don't pay for it sooner or later.

A Croat Among Jews

Nobody warned me what was waiting for me on my first trip to Israel, neither my Jewish friends, nor my Croatian friends. Perhaps they were not aware of it, or simply thought that I should have known, should have expected such a question to follow me there like a shadow: 'Do you feel guilty?'

As soon as I arrived at Tel Aviv Airport I realised that they don't see Croats there too often, except maybe on CNN. A policeman looked at my passport as if he were not quite sure what to do with it. 'This is the first Croatian passport I've seen,' he admitted. Even my hosts at the Van Leer Institute in Jerusalem, where I had been invited for a lecture, told me that they had very few chances to meet a Croat in their country. There is a technical explanation: that Israel and Croatia have not yet established diplomatic relations. I had had first-hand experience of what that actually means when the Israeli foreign ministry had to urge their own embassy in Stockholm to issue an entrance visa to me. This is because the Israeli government is basing its relationship with Croatia on the approximately 17,000

Jews (together with tens of thousands of Serbs, gipsies and Croat communists) exterminated in the Croatian concentration camp Jasenovac during the Second World War – that is, the Independent State of Croatia, one of the Nazi puppet states in Europe at that time. It is probably this that forced Israel to take a pro-Serbian stance during the recent war in the Balkans.

The second reason why Croats do not visit Israel very often I soon discovered for myself. Before my lecture, a benevolent professor, who introduced me to the public that night, told me that I should be prepared for pro-Serbian questions. In the event, the questions from the public were not particularly pro-Serbian, and certainly no different from those I have been asked in England, Sweden or the United States. They asked me whether the war had been caused by Germany recognising Croatia much too early; why the Croats had turned against the Muslims; what the Croats really had done in Krajina. All usual queries, I would say. But then I heard a female voice rising out of the darkness in front of me. 'Do you feel any regret?' she asked me. 'Do you feel guilty for what the Croats did to Jews during the war?'

The murmur in the audience stopped instantly. Suddenly, there was silence. I had the feeling that people were holding their breath for a moment. I was taken by surprise. Her voice sounded so young, I thought, as I scanned the audience for the questioner. She could not have been more than twenty, a student, perhaps. What could she have known about that time, about the holocaust, the feeling of guilt? Perhaps her grandmother or her grandfather, or some other relative, had ended his life as ashes or bones in Europe, maybe even in Jasenovac. But why was she asking me? What did I have to do with events that took place between 1941 and 1945, before I was even born?

The silence became too long. 'Yes,' I said at last. 'I am terribly sorry for what happened.' I phrased some kind of apology, saying that it could happen in any society or nation, that a handful of criminals could come to power and dishonour the country. 'But I can't say that I personally feel guilty because of that,' I added. 'I was born after the war, and my father was one of Tito's partisans and an anti-fascist, a member of the anti-fascist mass movement in the very same fascist state of Croatia. When discussing the role of Croatia during the war, perhaps we should not forget to mention that movement, too.' I also stressed that I was not a representative of the Croatian government or the Croatian people – whatever I said, it was on my own behalf only. Having made that clear, I believed that I had dealt with the question of guilt.

The next day I was invited, together with a few journalists and diplomats, to a dinner party at a journalist's house. We had barely finished the first course when a similar question hit me like a stone. To me it sounded as if someone had banged his fist on the table and cried, 'Enough of this pussyfooting around! First we will have to get the answer! So, do you feel guilty or not?' For some strange reason, perhaps because it was not a public occasion but a private dinner, I was again taken by surprise. For heaven's sake, is this matter of guilt always the first reaction of a Jew when he meets a Croat? As a Croat in Israel, was I supposed to constantly beat my breast, confessing to and apologising for something I myself had not done? I repeated what I had said the night before, but it seemed that the people around the table expected something more of me. I hesitate to use the word, but I felt they expected some kind of repentance. But I simply said that I had been born after the war, so how could I feel guilty?

Later that evening I learned that our hostess had survived Auschwitz as a young girl. Her friend had been saved from a similar destiny by a Dutch family, but her family had ended up in a concentration camp. Three other people at the dinner party had lost their relatives in the holocaust. Thus, that evening, I sat there directly confronting history. These very real people, with their own particular destinies, made me face, if not my own guilt, then at least the participation of my people in the crime of the extermination of the European Jews. In their presence my defence – the fact that I had not been born when it had all happened, was suddenly not strong enough.

During my stay in Israel, in conversations and meetings I had there, the mention of Croatian guilt on almost every occasion clung to me like a dark shadow. Otherwise amiable Jews would sooner or later stumble over the issue. And the journalists were the worst: they seemed to think it was the key not only to my country, but to myself as well. One from Ma'ariv was surprised at my lack of guilt; another, from the *Jerusalem Post*, tried to convince me that it was pretty normal for everyone to be asking me that question. But still I did not comprehend what they believed to be my personal guilt. Not until another young journalist from a Jerusalem weekly asked me, 'Is there any public discussion today about the guilt of the Croatian people during the war?' did I myself grasp what it was all about.

I finally understood that, in front of the victims and their relatives, it was much easier to defend yourself from the past than from the present. As far as the past was concerned, I could offer my regrets, but it was much more difficult to explain what the Croatian government and Croatian citizens were doing today to deal with that past. The Israelis were apparently very well informed: they knew about Franjo Tudjman's book and his claims minimising the number of Jews exterminated in Europe; they were aware that a member of Ante Pavelić's fascist government is now a member of the Croatian parliament, that streets are named after such people and that Croatian public opinion is more or less silent. I tried to explain that people in Croatia do not have many opportunities to state their opinions in newspapers because there is not much of a free press there. Besides, this issue in the new state of Croatia is not 'politically correct', and people are quite simply afraid to say what they think. They also have other, fresh crimes to deal with, too. But an even bigger problem is the fact that the government is not capable of clearly distancing itself from the crimes committed during the era of the fascist state. Indeed, according to the official interpretation, it seems to be more important that Croatia was an 'independent state' at that time rather than that it was a fascist creation – as if it were possible to separate those two elements of it.

When the young reporter's question brought me back into the present, I could not avoid my guilt any longer. What had bothered me before was that this guilt was somehow abstract, but now I realised that I had to deal with it not as an historical matter but in its present form. Every Croatian citizen bears a responsibility for his silent support of this government's attitude towards the holocaust. Why should I be exempted from such a responsibility? Why shouldn't Jews have the right to take up the rare opportunity to put such unpleasant questions to a Croat? To them, I was not only an individual, but also a citizen of Croatia. Whatever I might have felt about it, in their eyes I was defined by my connection to an historically incriminated nation. I had no excuse to avoid facing this history personally.

Yet something else bothered me. As much as I was surprised by Jews asking me about my guilt and the guilt of my people, I was bewildered by my own surprise. Why was I constantly astonished at the question? And why did I reproach the Jews for looking back to the past too much? They are trying to impose a feeling of guilt upon every single person, I told myself. Jews are good at blaming others, but look at what they are doing to the Palestinians! Besides, it is not only the Croats, but also the Austrians, the Slovaks, and even the French, who have not yet passed through any serious denazification. And anyway, I thought, how could they know what it means to have grown up under communism?

Of course they couldn't know. To grow up under communism means to live forever in the present. Once the final social order had been established, there was no need to look backwards – or forwards, for that matter. I had never understood the Latin phrase *historia est magistra vitae*. For us, for my generation, history was certainly not a teacher of life.

Perhaps this is the reason why we are now, with this recent war, sentenced to live in the past. Sometimes I ask myself whether this is the punishment for our lack of interest in history, for our fear, silence and irresponsibility towards ourselves. For our ignorance.

I had to visit Israel to understand that the past is not only a Jewish problem but ours, too. I had to answer their upsetting questions to realise that I must shoulder my part of the responsibility for today's attitude of the Croatian government towards the holocaust, fascism, and the rewriting of history. In the end I did feel my own responsibility, if not guilt. I had to, because I was morally squeezed into a corner. Today I am glad that I was.

Perhaps the difference between yesterday and today lies in the hope that history won't be for much longer a toy in the hands of a powerful few. When directly faced with the question of personal responsibility, a person cannot view history as a series of incomprehensible acts of a leader or a government. Eventually he must understand that it also depends upon what he himself says and does. In post-communist Croatia, we don't have a good excuse for our silence any more.

My Father's Guilt

My father was a nobody. He was one of the poor devils who fought with Tito's partisan army during the Second World War; later on, he joined the Communist Party of Yugoslavia and became an army officer, retiring in 1966. His life is not much of a story, and he is dead now. He died in November 1989, just before his world and the ideas he fought for fell apart, which, perhaps, would have ended his life anyway. He may not have been an important figure in the communist *nomenklatura*, but in my eyes my father was guilty of opportunism, of a tacit collaboration with a repressive regime, and above all of silence.

But so was the majority of the 20 million people of the former Yugoslavia, and of the 5 million people in Croatia, for that matter.

My father was born in 1922. I have only two photographs of him taken before the war. One of them, perhaps the first ever taken of him, shows him as a boy of five, posing with his older brother and his mother. The second must have been taken when he was about fifteen, at the wedding of a relative. He is wearing a suit. The sleeves of the jacket are too short, and I would guess that he borrowed it from a friend for the occasion. These two photographs speak the same language to me, the language of poverty. My father's father was a bricklayer from a little town near Rijeka, who died before his fortieth birthday. His mother worked in a factory and sold vegetables grown on her small piece of land at the market. Yet my father was a spoiled child; he would eat all the food in the house and destroy a new pair of shoes within a week, playing football. His dream was to have a bicycle of his own, and he practically forced his mother to buy him one, even though she had to borrow the money to pay for it. My father became a carpenter, but he did not like his job. Life was somewhere else, downtown, where there were beautiful houses, cars, good shoes, good suits.

In 1941, when the war broke out, his brother joined the 'people's army'. Not long afterwards, my father went into the woods himself. I doubt that he knew exactly why. You could say that he preferred to join the partisan army to defend his homeland against the German and Italian fascists to being drafted into the fascist army of Ante Pavelić's Independent State of Croatia (NDH). Of course, later on he claimed that this was exactly the case, because then it was the right thing to say. But it is hard to know if he did it out of patriotism and ideology; it could just as well have been a coincidence. Perhaps he did it because his brother and his pals had joined Tito, and not the other side. Coincidence or not, it decided his whole life.

I know very little about this part of his life, and today I think I know too little about his life in general. I did not ask. I was born in 1949 and everything before that seemed to belong to a pre-history that had nothing to do with my life. The little I know I learned from his mother, who followed her sons and cooked for the partisan army. I know that he became a *politkom*, a political commissar in charge of ideological matters; that he once narrowly escaped being executed by his comrades for having stolen a piece of cheese from a peasant's house; that he survived typhoid fever and a long march during which most of his comrades-in-arms froze to death.

The first photograph of him after the war, taken in 1945, shows a self-assured young man dressed in a somewhat shabby uniform. The course his life then took was a mixture of ideology, poverty and opportunism – approximately the same combination that ruled the lives of most people in Yugoslavia at that time. In some cases there was a little less ideology than opportunism, in others vice versa, but the result was pretty much the same for everyone: the kind of life we all had in the ensuing forty-five years. During the war, my father had become a member of the Communist Party and he did not want to go back to being a carpenter. He took the chance offered to stay in the army as an officer, attended the military academy, got married and started a family.

My memory finds us in a two-roomed apartment in Senj, where my father was in charge of the army headquarters, in the early fifties. There is another picture of him to remind me of those years: a New Year celebration. It must have been New Year 1953 or 1954. He is sitting at a table with his colleagues, again in uniform, but this time a well-tailored and more elegant one. I remember that particular black and white photo for one reason: that table, with what seemed like masses of food on it, with cakes and fruits. It is also where I first saw an orange – right there, in the middle of the table, peeled and sliced into pieces. When he brought the photograph home, I asked him what it was. An orange, my father said; an orange, I repeated, memorising the name of the mysterious fruit which, in that instant, became a symbol of wealth to me. But the word itself did not mean much until, a long time later, I tasted that strange, sweet-smelling fruit, connected to that picture of my father forever.

We bought our first record-player in 1963 – it was a birthday present for my mother – our first black and white TV set two years later, and then our very first car, a second-hand VW Rabbit. In the early seventies my parents started to build a weekend house, but by that time my father was in poor health and growing disappointed that our society was not working as it should. He was one of those people who believed in the system itself; it was not working only because the wrong people were in the wrong places, doing the wrong things. But I had already decided that my life had nothing to do with my father's life and his opinions, much less with his past. I was not a communist; on the contrary, I became staunchly anti-communist because of him. My father was a very authoritarian man, and at the age of sixteen, I rejected his whole system of values and beliefs, along with his authority, and ran away from home. He never forgave me for that, and so we did not have much chance to talk to each other before the end of his days.

I was stupid and stubborn, and I regret this today, especially when I visit his grave. He was buried in a small graveyard on an island in the northern Adriatic. When I sit there, looking at the beautiful bay, I sometimes feel that he should have given me the opportunity to talk to him about the important issues of the past. But in any case these questions became important only after the outbreak of the war in Croatia in 1991, and by that time he was long dead.

When I visit his grave I get sad, but also upset and angry at the same time. On his tombstone, under his name, there is an engraved star. My mother instructed a stonemason to put it there because, after all, my father had been a communist and an opponent of fascism, and that star was a part of his life. But soon I noticed that my mother was covering it up with a wreath of flowers. At first I thought it was accidental, but once, when we visited the graveyard together, I removed the wreath because it looked worn out, and without a word, she put it back again. Only then did I understand: the newspapers were full of stories about demolished partisan monuments, about changed street names, about people renouncing their communist past. Already some graves had been desecrated, people had been evicted from military apartments, widows of former Yugoslav federal army officers were being threatened. The big ideological 'cleansing' of the past was well underway. In the new dictionary of 'political correctness', the recent communist era in Yugoslavia was nothing but a 'bloody dictatorship' or a 'concentration camp'; at the very least a dark period of history. The message was clear: anyone who had had anything to do with it had better hide their connections. My mother was afraid my father's grave would be desecrated: his tombstone was the only one in the cemetery with a star instead of a cross. What could she do but cover it up?

I was upset; I thought that her gesture was pathetic, for everyone in the small town knew the star was there and there was therefore no point in hiding it. But as much as I didn't like her insecurity, I could understand it, and her fear of the new political climate. A feeling of fury overwhelmed me: standing at the graveyard I could see that someone was stealing the past away from my father, from me, from all of us, and we were just letting it happen – more than that, we even eagerly co-operated in this robbery, in order to cover the traces of the recent past in our own lives. We shut out our memories, closing our eyes as well as our mouths. We collaborated with new political forces, making it easier for them to rewrite history as they pleased, to falsify it and to finally erase it. We thought that we could change the colour of our skin like a chameleon.

I know where my anger came from. It came from the fact that I could not help but identify my mother's action with what is going on in our society today, and it had to do not only with the red star or communism, but also, and more importantly, with the way we relate to our own past. My father does not deserve to have the star on his tomb covered, nor does my mother deserve the fear she feels in the new Croatian state. This is not only because my father was my father and I care about him, but because he lived his life no differently from most other people, sharing the same ideology and benefiting from it in the same way. If his life is to be denied, they too must accept the denial of their own past in the name of the new political reality, which for them must be a much more difficult and devastating operation, since they are still alive.

Moreover, it should not be forgotten that my father, along with hundreds of thousands of others, was part of the anti-fascist movement which in the Second World War determined the future of Europe, and put Croatia on the winning side. The star under his name stands for that, too.

But because my father participated in creating communism in Yugoslavia, his life is now disappearing along with the political system itself. You don't need to be a communist to feel that there is injustice being done, not only to my father and people like him, but to the rest of us, too. If we remember only too well the bad side of living in Yugoslavia during the last forty-five years, perhaps we should also have the courage to recall things like the much higher standard of living and greater freedom we enjoyed than did the rest of the communist states. We had refrigerators and washing machines when others did not, and could travel abroad, see American movies, buy a graduation dress in Milan or spend our summer holidays in Greece or Spain. Yes, essentially it is a comparison between prison cells, but the comfort of your cell makes a lot of difference when you are imprisoned. Today, no one could tell me that it made no difference at all, or that Yugoslavia under Tito was the same totalitarian country as the rest in the *Lager*. Such a person would not have a clue what he is talking about.

One of the most beautiful squares in Zagreb still bears Tito's name. I say still, because it will be only a matter of time before it is changed. A couple of years ago, the Commission for the Renaming of Streets proposed that it should be named after Ante Pavelić, but someone up there in the city council, or even higher, decided that it would be an act of overt rehabilitation of the fascist leader of the NDH (the Nazi puppet state from 1941 to 1945). Most certainly, it would have harmed the image of the new state, which could not afford to antagonise its allies, so the change was postponed until better times. When Tito loses his beautiful square, he will probably get a smaller one, and the new name of 'his' square is not yet known. In the meantime, however, a process of more subtle affirmation of the fascist period – which, to complicate matters even more, corresponds with the establishment of the first Croatian independent state – goes on uninterrupted.

For there is more to this purge than the blowing up, destroying or tucking away of communist and anti-fascist monuments; more than the removal of memorial plaques from buildings and walls. There is also the visible, although not official, celebration of 10 April, the day of the birth of the fascist state, the naming of streets and schools after Mile Budak, who indeed was a writer, but also a minister of culture and education in Pavelić's government who personally signed racist anti-Jewish laws. There is the naming of Croatian army brigades after Ustashe war criminals, and graffiti in Split that says: 'Death to the Jews', which has been there for a year now. There is the flood of history books telling the 'truth' about the heroic role of Ante Pavelić, and the naming of the new currency: now it is called the *kuna*, just as it was in the days of the fascist state. The list is endless.

I have no doubts that if things continue like this, Pavelić will have his square sooner rather than later. In the preamble of the new constitution it is explicitly stated that the new independent republic of Croatia is founded on the traditions of the anti-fascist movement. In practice, however, this means nothing. Though he is an anti-fascist and communist himself, our President is paying only lip service to this tradition, and even then only when he is obliged to do so. How can we believe what he says about the importance of opposing fascism when Vinko Nikolić, a high-ranking former official in the fascist Croatian state, is sitting right there in the Parliament, being publicly congratulated on his birthday by the President?

Of course, Tito did have far too many streets and squares and schools and bridges, and even several towns, named after him. Not to mention all those portraits, hanging in every office and every classroom. On the photograph we had during my days in the first grade, he wore a white uniform. It must have been rather old, because all colours were hand-painted and the unknown photographer had put great effort into painting his cheeks very pink, his eyes bright blue and his lips red, which only made him look more surrealistic, like a transvestite. Now President Tudjman's picture hangs in exactly the same places, but it is some comfort to know that he, at least, has been elected. Tito has lost all his pictures, squares and streets; soon he will be swallowed up by oblivion, until the moment when he comes back to trouble us as a restless ghost.

In 1994 I read in the Croatian newspapers an 'open letter to the Croatian people' from the Party of the Right (HSP), considered to be on the extreme right of the Croatian political spectrum. It is a protest against the naming of another square in Zagreb after Tito, on the grounds that this 'offends the blood, tears and suffering of the Croatian people'. There follows a list of accusations against Tito, from falsification of history to the killing of priests and the biological genocide of the Croatian people in favour of the Serbs. The letter concludes that the Croatian people have no reason to publicly honour Josip Broz Tito and his followers, who 'for fifty years exercised a kind of terror that Croatia cannot remember throughout her history'. Those who dare suggest that his name should be given to another square in Zagreb are enemies of the independence of the new Croatian state, Bolsheviks who call themselves anti-fascists. Such a public honour should be given to those people who distinguished themselves in the struggle for 'the wellbeing of that [Croatian] people, especially in the struggle for survival, freedom and state independence'.

Unfortunately, in this part of the world it all depends upon a pretty arbitrary interpretation of the 'wellbeing' of one nation or the state. I am afraid that in most cases such an interpretation is usually the result of the latest political and ideological twists, and not of a cool and rational insight into our history and the true merits of this or that man. Of course, such a letter of protest from the party of the extreme right is only to be expected, and I don't see it as a cause for alarm. But what makes it significant is that the government acts exactly according to this kind of accusation against Tito, and Tito does not have the benefit of a public trial.

The problem with Tito is in essence the same as the problem with my father: he was a communist, but he was an opponent of fascism too. Of course, Tito was much more than that, and therefore he is more responsible and more guilty than my father was. He was a dictator, but at the same time he was a capable soldier and later a statesman who succeeded in leading Yugoslavia out of the Soviet camp. He was also a crook who borrowed money everywhere and left his country with enormous foreign debts, but as a result people lived a relatively comfortable life. He was responsible for the massacre of war prisoners at Bleiburg and forced labour camps such as Goli Otok, for political prisoners and the violation of human rights. But it is to his credit that Yugoslavia was not an isolated communist 'gulag'. Yet, his name is disappearing from public view and from history itself, with no one daring to defend his obvious merits.

It is clear that the Croats have, to put it euphemistically, a problem with accepting their own past. All I am saying is this: before finally condemning Tito to, in Marx's own words, the 'lumber room of history', we should at least have a proper (that is, free) discussion about who he really was and what were his historical merits as well as his crimes. Even during the Stalinist show trials, a culprit had the right, albeit not a practicable one, to a defence. Without trying to evaluate Tito's role in history, by demonising him instead, and to the point where his name represents an offence against the new Croatian state, we are falsifying the past – just as the communists did when they came to power.

Falsification of history, denial of memories, ideological arguments for reinterpreting historical events – all of this had happened before, and not so long ago. In 1947 the communist government removed a statue of Duke Jelačić from the main square in Zagreb and renamed it the Square of the Republic. Some forty-five years later, the new non-communist government returned the statue of Duke Jelačić to the square and gave it back its old name, despite the fact that there can be nothing wrong with such an innocuous name as the Square of the Republic, except that it was given by communists. It might even seem that through such an act 'historical justice' has finally been exercised, were it not that new injustices of the same kind are happening daily.

All this reveals a deeply rooted disease of repeating our past. What, in fact, is our perception of the nature of history? Judging from this kind of experience, we seem to be convinced that history is a bottomless pit, a black hole into which one throws one's past when it is no longer needed. We actually seem to believe that it is possible to forget our own past and leave our guilt behind with it. It is history as a washing machine: you throw in your dirty laundry, add a little ideology as detergent, and out comes a bright, clean, almost new shirt, ready to wear until it gets dirty again.

I must say that I am tired of this game, which I know all too well: one day a new leader shows up and orders the elimination of those who came before him. After forty-five years another leader takes his place, ordering his predecessor to be erased. And you can be sure that in two or three generations, a third leader will pop up, wiping out the memory of the latter and rehabilitating the former.

A friend of mine told me that after the communists came into power and changed all the names of the streets and squares in Zagreb, her grandmother continued to use the old names throughout her life. She did not accept the new names, even if it led to confusion. It was the price she was willing to pay in order to preserve the memory of her own life before communism. The old lady lived long enough to see old names restored, but she was perfectly aware that in the meantime her life did not halt. In forty-five years she had grown old and had become a grandmother, and then a great-grandmother. She'd shrunk, she'd almost lost her hearing and her eyes had become very weak.

Should those forty-five years of her life – a real, concrete, palpable life – end up, disdained and forgotten, in the 'lumber room of history', without the right to be remembered? Or should she be entitled to keep the memory of that time alive, in her family album as well as in a museum, or even through the name of a square? Who has the right to decide this on her behalf. Of course, I am not suggesting that we should follow her example and continue to call streets after this or that partisan brigade or hero; what I mean is that while the existence of the new state should be respected, so too should our history.

The same feeling I experience at my father's grave comes over me when I stand at the former Square of Victims of Fascism, now the Square of Croatia's Great Men (this new name is completely pointless and irritating – if they are great, why are they anonymous?). On the square, facing south, there is a grim, grey five-storey building, formerly the notorious fascist prison where thousands of people were tortured, among them writers and poets. In a way, it is also a symbolic graveyard, not only of the victims, but of our illusions about the new government. For in spite of all the protests, the name of the square was taken away. Again, I feel frustrated, as if by removing the old nameplate someone has stolen a part of my own history, my own identity. I stand there like an abandoned child. I know that I am forty-five years old and that this sounds ridiculous, but it is how I feel. I feel helpless. I feel as if I have missed something. I feel as if I'll never have a chance to grow up because history is closing yet another chapter right here.

Looking at the former Square of Victims of Fascism reminds me of my own guilt. And then a picture of my father emerges again. This time it is not a photograph of him, although it could easily be one, so still and frozen does it lie in my memory. My brother and I were children when, one day, we found a pistol hidden in our father's cupboard. As we looked at it, the door opened and my father entered the room. He took the pistol away from us and told us never to play with it again. What has stayed with me all these years is the look on his face. His face was very pale, immobile. His eyes had no expression – they were like two empty holes. For a moment, he looked as if he had seen a ghost of someone long dead and forgotten, someone he had not believed would ever appear again. He was frightened, I instinctively sensed that, and I felt that his fear was infecting me, too.

Many times afterwards I wanted to ask my father what he had seen at that moment. Death? But whose death was it? Had he ever killed a man with that pistol during the war? Whom did he kill, and why? If I had had the courage to ask him that, perhaps later I would have been able to ask him other questions, too. But every time I had it on the tip of my tongue, I could not bring myself to actually utter it. While he still was alive I did not know why this was. Now that he is dead, I realise that I was paralysed by the fear of what his answer might be. I know that if my father had said he had killed somebody, something would have cracked inside me. In my eyes, he would never have been the same person again. Yes, I was afraid of the truth. I could not face it. I pushed that question deep into my subconscious. And he made it easy for me. On the rare occasions when we would stumble upon it, he used to tell me that I did not need to know about the war, because something like that would never happen again. My God, what made him so sure of that? That's what I would like to ask him today. But from then on, I silently accepted his silence.

I have a lot of excuses handy for not asking questions that I should have asked. For example, I could say that my generation, born after the war, was cynical and apolitical. It would be the truth, but not the whole truth. Perhaps this attitude towards life and politics was a kind of escapism, as we saw that we had no chance of any power ourselves. As in all other communist countries, gerontocracy ruled and younger generations were totally infantilised. Somehow, they were always too young to climb high or to reach responsible positions. These eternal children could not even hope for an apartment of their own. Instead, they would grow up and have their own children in their parents' apartment, never even being able to break out of the circle of power within the family. The other side of this coin was lack of responsibility, for no one demanded or expected it of us. If something in society went wrong, a father figure was expected to deal with it, not a son. The ultimate result was a kind of bargain: give us a taste of freedom (the chance to travel to the West, good clothes, books and records) and we won't make any problems for you. We won't ask unpleasant questions.

I think that the majority of my generation truly believed in oblivion and obedience in exchange for what they thought was a good life. Yes, it was opportunism. Moreover, I think it was not much different from the kind of opportunism that probably made my father join the communist party. I personally was arrogant enough to think that a real life in communist Yugoslavia had nothing to do with my inner self, my personality, my dreams and values. I did not believe in the Marxist formula that circumstances determine character – quite the contrary. It sounds terrible, I know, but it is only now that I realise that the majority of us were true believers in communism. Infantilised, pampered and bribed, we did not believe in the possibility of a different future. We could not imagine a future outside the communist context that sheltered our childish dreams, in the same way as a child is not able to conceive of life outside his own playground. The price of this was high, and I think we are paying it now.

I believe that we can't just forget, but we have to deal with our recent communist past, as well as our fascist past. It is all part of our identity and of our growing up as individuals, as citizens, and, for that matter, as a nation. It is essential if we decide that we don't want to repeat the same mistakes that brought us where we are now – to the war. Besides, I am convinced that in dealing with the past we should focus less on other people's guilt and more on our own. Perhaps this is what I would like to tell my father today – to tell him, not to ask him any more. It is too easy to blame someone else – my father, our fathers, Tito, the system. What have I done myself that gives me the right to question other people's moral or political responsibility?

Neither I nor others of my generation have been able to predict, or to prevent, or even to work against the war that is going on now. I am afraid that, in the eyes of my daughter and her generation, who are fighting this war and dying, I am indeed the responsible one.

It would be easier, I imagine, if this feeling of guilt could be attached only to the past. But the same kind of guilt is being created again – my own, that of my generation and that of all the people living in my country. The trouble is not that the new government would like to make us all forget the recent past and live happily ever after, in spite of the fact that it is more or less discreetly establishing a direct link with the 1941–45 period, thus rehabilitating fascism. The trouble is that we are showing our tacit acceptance of these changes, as if they did not relate to our own lives, our own future. Yet again someone is deciding our past and our present, and we are enduring and obeying. There is no other excuse but fear – and I admit that it is a powerful enough excuse to make us close our eyes and shut up. But shouldn't we ask ourselves about the nature of that fear? If we excuse ourselves in front of our children for being silent in the past, because we lived in a dictatorship, what do we do now? Do we dare to confess that we feel fear in a democracy, too – and if so, what kind of democracy is that?

To forget, how sweet it must be to be able to really forget. Perhaps that is how eternity feels. We would have to ask Tito about that. Ironically, it was he who inaugurated the principle of erasing the past. We saw it during his lifetime as well as after his death. According to his own wish, Tito's tomb of white marble in Belgrade does not have a star engraved on it. By this decision he had already deleted his own communist and anti-fascist past, ten years before it started to happen in this part of the world. This, and only this, would be my personal reason not to give his name to a square in Zagreb, because I can almost hear him laughing in his immaculate grave. But he deserves it nonetheless. By denying Tito this memorial, we deny a part of our history that nevertheless exists. It is still there, in people's minds, in the way they think and behave. The important thing is that we finally learn not to take orders. This is where my father's guilt meets my own – both of us have been too good at that.

People from the Three Borders

I have a house in Istria. It is situated on the top of a hill, in what once used to be a little medieval town. The view from the hill stretches out almost to the sea in the south, almost to Trieste in the west, to the stony plateau of Ćićarija in the north and finally to the big mountain of Učka in the east. When I am there I often have the feeling that I am on the bridge of a ship, especially when, in autumn, a milky fog covers everything except the surrounding hilltops, giving them the appearance of islands.

But I am not on a ship. My house is in the middle of a peninsula in the northern Adriatic, between the bay of Trieste and the bay of Rijeka. Since the collapse of Yugoslavia, the biggest part of the peninsula belongs to Croatia, the smaller part to Slovenia, but there is also a tiny little strip of land that belongs to Italy. Thus the 4,500 square kilometres of the peninsula are divided among three states, I live in one, and I can almost see the other two from my window.

Every time I climb the hill to my house I am happy. But

as soon as I turn my eyes away from the beautiful landscape, reminiscent of Tuscany, my mood turns gloomy. I become aware of questions I don't like, of pressures I don't feel anywhere else. First of all, I become acutely aware of the new borders. When I descend from Črni Kal to Sočerga, from the mountains to the valley, the landscape does not change, people understand each other's languages and eat the same food, but everything is overshadowed by a newly erected monster – the iron construction called the state border that divides them. The real border here was installed by nature itself, because this is the point where the Mediterranean culture begins, the culture of olive oil, wine, fish, pasta and several languages that one assimilates just by being born here.

The sea is no more than 50 or 60 kilometres away in any direction from the heart of Istria, and it brings an openness to the atmosphere, the food and the habits of the people.

At the state border Slovenes nonchalantly wave you through, without even looking at your passport. But on the other side the Croats are waiting. You can see the suspicion in their eyes when they ask you if you have anything to declare. Myself, I'm always tempted to answer, but instead I say nothing. I feel as if I am sinking into a different reality, not a visible one, but no less real for that. I was born in Rijeka, a city that shared some of the history of the peninsula. The city itself was divided during the Second World War. My mother lived in Sušak (which belonged to Yugoslavia) and worked in Rijeka (which belonged to Italy). Every single day she crossed the bridge in the middle of the city that separated the two countries from each other. I too feel the burden of the question that Istrians are asked today: who are you? Not in the metaphysical sense, but in a very concrete one. People are asked that directly or indirectly. It means are you Croat? Are you a proper Croat? Are you patriotic enough – that is, are you a nationalist?

Istria is the most western part of Croatia, the most southern part of Slovenia and the most north-eastern part of Italy. It is on the edge of each of these countries, as it used to be on the edge of the Austro–Hungarian empire or Yugoslavia. The pressure to define, to categorise, to choose one particular nationality has been here before, and the same practice is part of the new political reality. Once again, the 300,000 people living on the three borders are pressed to prove their national affiliations, as people from the margins of any state always have to do in turbulent times. These demands bring insecurity and fear. There may be no war here, but there is no peace either.

Going from Buzet to Trieste, you have to show your passport four times in the course of a journey that takes little more than half an hour – and you have to cross another state, Slovenia, in the process. You might work in one town while your wife works in another, perhaps only a ten-minute drive away, but in Slovenia. You might wake up every morning and go to dig your potatoes in a field on the other side of the border. Istria is a rather small and compact geographical unit, and because of that, borders here have always been intangible. There was no iron curtain here: people got married, worked and lived together, not only across the Croatian–Slovenian border, but also across the Yugoslav–Italian one. Now that a real border has been erected, in the first place between Croatia and Slovenia, you become aware of just how small Istria is. This partition is the consequence of a political decision, not of the way people here live.

Istria is a territory of ten distinctly different Slavic dialects and four dialects of Italian origin. Yet if you enter a bar or a village shop, you will be addressed in your own language while the barman or shopkeeper and other customers continue to chat among themselves in another, and perhaps even a third as well. At my friend Igor's house, his parents talk to him in a Croatian language and to his wife in Italian. This happens at the kitchen table, during the same conversation, while they all eat the same minestrone soup and drink the same sour Merlot wine. They switch languages with no visible effort, understanding each other perfectly. This mixture of languages and the ease with which the people slip from one into the other is characteristic of life here. People understand each other on a deeper level. They do not make problems out of their differences; it is others who do that.

This part of Croatia is today a problematic region. When in 1994 a Croat reporter interviewed inhabitants of three Croatian border villages which had been annexed overnight by Slovenes, he was faced with a 'strange' reaction. To the Croat reporter, these people said that they were Croats, to Italian reporters that they were, of course, Italians, and the Slovene reporters were told they were Slovenes. They would say the same to any representative of officialdom. 'Who are they really?' the confused journalists asked. But the locals saw no contradiction in claiming three different nationalities; neither would they describe themselves as opportunists. In their view, the misunderstanding lies in the fact that the journalists were posing a simple 'either–or' type of question. To the reporters, it was impossible for one person to be a Croat, an Italian and a Slovene all at the same time. The journalists saw the villagers' nationalities as political categories; the villagers were talking about their own identity, of which their nationalities were only one aspect.

Indeed, nationality and identity don't necessarily overlap, and perhaps Istria is the best example of this. If it was only journalists who were taking an interest in nationality as a political category it would not be much of a problem, but there are others, too, namely, the centralist government in Zagreb. They want to know who the hell those people in Istria are. When the majority of Croatian citizens voted for an independent state of Croatia in 1990, why, in the census of 1991, did as many as 20 per cent of them declare themselves Istrians and not Croats? Istrians were a non-existent category in the census and this 20 per cent should have listed themselves under 'others'.

But Istrians today are apparently trying to establish their region as their 'nationality', because they want to avoid defining themselves, or being defined by others, as 'pure' Croats, or Italians, or Slovenes, or Serbs. Zagreb is, of course, right to suspect them of not being nationalistic enough, as are Ljubljana or Rome. Sitting there ruling from hundreds of kilometres away, how can these authorities understand the meaning of Istrianism – the enlarging concept of identity, as opposed to the reducing concept of nationality? To Istrians, identity is broader and deeper than nationality, and they cannot choose a single 'pure' nationality as their identity. Living in the border region, they understand better than anyone else that we all have mixed blood to a greater or lesser extent. They have also suffered from nationalism, and in its worst form – ethnic cleansing – enough to have grown tired of it. Paradoxically, for the first time in their history, at the first elections of the newly independent republic of Croatia, the Istrians felt free to reject the concept of one nation; they felt that the time had come to express what they really consider themselves to be. But in today's nationalist Croatia, this was not what was expected of them.

My nearest neighbour is Karlo, or Carletto – two names for the same sixty-seven-year-old man with thick glasses and a bad leg. Whether he is Karlo or Carletto depends on whether he is sober or not. In the morning he declares himself a Croat, speaks a bad Croatian dialect and is prepared to enter any political debate, if he is not too preoccupied by the weather. But he is only a Croat until early afternoon. By then, he has consumed several glasses of cognac and enough beer in the local bar to assume his other, Italian nationality. Now he is Carletto. Suddenly, he speaks an equally bad Italian dialect, remembering episodes from his youth under both the Italian fascist government and, later, the Yugoslav communist one. To complicate matters further, his younger brother opted for Italy during the referendum after the end of the Second World War. This man lives in Trieste and visits his elder brother once a month. Their sister lives in a small town in the Croatian part of Istria.

Again, Karlo–Carletto, in common with all the people from the three villages, sees no contradiction in being both Croat and Italian, not even in the space of a single day. Moreover, he is both at the same time, and each of these nationalities is part of his identity. If you ask him to choose just one, he can't do it, because he would have to choose between his brother and his sister, between his father and his mother. All his life he has lived in a small, long deserted and decayed village, where one cannot even buy newspapers. He does not drive, he has no television (although he listens to the radio) and he ascends to the nearby town only when he needs a doctor. All his life he has been only himself. Why would he want to pick out one part of himself and confine his identity to that one trait? As we have seen, lately, he and many others in Istria have formulated their protest against the political pressure of the 'purists' by declaring themselves Istrians, which has driven the Croatian Democratic Union ruling party leaders, party apparatchiks, and especially hard-core nationalists crazy. This has had direct political implications. In the first elections, the population of Istria voted overwhelmingly (68 per cent) for its regional party, thus defeating the centralist right-wing CDU in the region. In the last elections, in 1995, the regional party won an even bigger victory: this time it got 77 per cent of the votes. The message is clear. *You tell us it is impossible and politically incorrect for us to declare ourselves Istrians, that is regionalists. Well, we'll show you exactly what it means to us: it means subordinating any nation and ideology to the region; it means that identity rates higher than nationality, because nationality reduces you to one political dimension only, while identity encompasses your whole human experience.* In fact, what started as a psychological defence mechanism against nationalism has developed into a political project.

Clearly, Istrianism is a reaction to the long historical experience of the people living here. And this was always a region not only of mixed population, but also of a shifting one. For example, in the census of 1910, 39 per cent of the people in Istria were Italians, 50 per cent of them Slavs (Croats and Slovenes). Under Benito Mussolini's fascist government, 30,000 to 40,000 more Italians arrived from Italy, while there was an exodus of part of the Croatian population for fear of fascism. The other big exodus took place after the Second World War, when half the population – mostly Italians, but also many Croats – fled Istria, afraid of the revenge of Tito's communists. The peninsula has never recovered from that loss. People literally left everything behind, cows and pigs in the stables, even food cooking on the stoves. The communist government confiscated their property. Despite the Osimo Treaty between Yugoslavia and Italy, signed in the seventies, which supposedly solved this problem, their property is still a difficult issue and can always be used as an argument to start a conflict. The result is that today only about 8 per cent of the people living in the Croatian part of Istria are Italians.

The departure of both Italians and Slavs was the result of nationalist ideologies and of 'ethnic cleansing', of forced Italianisation as well as forced Slavisation. That particular experience – shifting populations, shifting governments and shifting borders – has forged the Istrian identity. The Istrians of today have learned to tolerate different languages and nations, to live together irrespective of political borders and to put their region above nation or ideology. The Istrian model has demonstrated that tolerance is possible, and that it works. Yet today's Croatia, with its tendency towards a nation state, views this as a problem, not a success story. An alternative based on values other than nationalism is automatically suspect.

To go shopping in Trieste is quite normal here. You would think that it would be the norm to go to Rijeka, because the distance is the same and you don't have to pass any state borders, and the language is Croatian there. But this is not the logic in Istria, and the reason is simple. During communism, people went to Trieste because in Yugoslavia there was not much to buy. Nowadays, they go because there is still a better choice, *and* everything is cheaper. As I have mentioned one of the paradoxes of the post-communist economy is that the same goods are more expensive in, say, Croatia, Slovenia or Albania than they are in Italy, Germany or even Austria. It is enough to visit one shop in Rijeka and one in Trieste to compare prices, and you will have no doubts about where to go shopping.

On one weekly food-shopping excursion to Trieste I took a friend along, a neighbour from my little town up in the hills. As we approached the Croatian state border, he took out his Croatian passport. But on entering Slovenia, he showed a Slovenian passport to the police officer. To my surprise, this was not the end of the story: when we reached Italy, he produced a third document, a brand-new Italian passport! I asked him why he possessed three passports. 'It is a matter of survival; one never knows what will happen here,' he answered simply. I was interested in how he had acquired them all. He was born in Croatia, so here he got the Croatian passport. But he had also worked for a long time in Slovenia, and this gave him the right to claim a Slovenian passport, too. But what about the Italian one? In February 1992, the Italian parliament passed a new law on citizenship, which made it possible for those Istrians who had not taken the opportunity to opt for Italy before 1955, and who had therefore been Yugoslavian citizens, to regain their Italian citizenships if they applied within two years. This particular law caused an outcry in Croatia, because it was interpreted as a scheme to reconquer Istria. But the Istrians themselves took it rather pragmatically, as one might expect. It gave them the chance of an Italian pension, of a job there if there were no jobs in Istria, and to educate their children in Italy, all of which doesn't necessarily make them Italians, much less traitors, as they have been portrayed in the official press in Croatia. The way my friend sees it, his identity is not defined by changing his nationality from one to another, or again to a third, but in incorporating all of them. He, too, is a strong regionalist and is an advocate of transregionalism, the practice of economically connecting parts of the same geographic area across state borders. To Zagreb, of course, this sounds like yet another threat from the people of the three borders.

Yet most of all, my friend would prefer to get rid of all of his passports. He is well aware that in today's united Europe it is archaic to put up new borders and to have three passports instead of one. 'Imagine,' he says to me, 'one day, perhaps only a few years from now, both Slovenia and Croatia will become members of the European Union. All these papers and tensions, all our fears and insecurity, will suddenly become obsolete. And no one will force us to identify with just one part of what we experience as our identity. I dream about that day, when nobody will hate me because of the food I prefer, my memory, or the language I speak.'

I know what he means. I remember driving from Austria to Italy for the first time after the Austrians entered the EU. I remember my excitement when I saw the empty, abandoned crossing point near Villach, the vacant sentry boxes and the absence of customs. But being a part of Croatia – that is, of the disunited part of Europe – before entering such a bright future, both Istrians and all other Croatians will be forced to live not in the present, but in the past, for yet some time to come.

He Sleeps Like a Baby

It is Easter 1945. As the man and his wife step out
of their house on the hillside in a northern part
of Zagreb, a camera clicks.

Who took that picture? Was it a friend who just
happened to be there, or perhaps the man's adjutant, whose
job included taking photographs? Perhaps it was simply a
neighbour. The identity of the photographer is not important. I can imagine the young couple – for he was twenty-
four years old at the time and she must have been even
younger – standing in front of number 94 Pantovčak at that
moment, already smelling the spring in the air. She is
elegantly and solemnly dressed in a dark, two-piece suit
ornamented with traditional embroidery, her thick, brown
hair falling over her shoulders. She looks into the camera
with a trace of a confused smile. She is not exactly a beauty,
but with her skirt a little above her knees, she looks very
modern. Yet her whole posture reveals hesitation, as if she
is not sure what to do, because she is not pleased to be
photographed at that particular moment. No, the two of
them are definitely not posing – I can detect it in his face,

too. Standing half in profile, he looks away from the camera. He does not care about the photographer or about the impression he will give – he has something else on his mind. He, too, is elegantly dressed, in the uniform of an army officer of the Independent State of Croatia (NDH), complete with a sable. It is not likely that this couple are heading off to an officers' ball or a merry party at a friend's house. They both look quite distressed. It must be a more serious occasion. Perhaps an intimate dinner with General Maks Luburić, their close relative, or a meeting with the head of the state, Ante Pavelić, whose exclusive confidence this man enjoys?

This photograph was taken only a couple of weeks before this young officer's relative and superior, General Luburić, ordered him to flee Zagreb, which he did on 7 May 1945. Therefore, it is possible that the young man already knows about the order, or suspects that it will come. Perhaps the news was to be conveyed to him that very evening, as he must have been aware that the end of the NDH state was only a matter of days away. As Pavelić's confidant, he must have known that he, too, was secretly preparing to flee from Tito's army. In fact that army entered Zagreb on 8 May 1945 – the Day of Freedom, later celebrated as a holiday until the break-up of communist Yugoslavia. This is undoubtedly the explanation for his somewhat troubled air.

The man in the photograph is Dinko Šakić. At Easter 1945, he was a high-ranking officer in the NDH army hierarchy. He also had very good contacts, being married to the sister of his superior, General Maks Luburić, the chief commander of the concentration camps, as well as being Pavelić's right hand. Dinko Šakić was born in 1921 to a Croat family in Herzegovina. He was an early school drop-out, and after a problematic youth, he joined the Ustashe army in Jasenovac in 1941. Soon he was transferred to another, smaller concentration camp in Stara Gradiška, where he served as assistant to its commander. In 1942 he returned to the Jasenovac camp as its vice-commander, and later its commander.

Jasenovac concentration camp was not forced upon the Croatian state by Nazi Germany, it was a product of the politics and ideology of the Croatian fascist government itself. Historians today do not dispute the fact that the mass murders of Serbs, Jews, Croatian communists and gipsies actually took place, but there is argument about how many people were executed there – calculations vary from 30,000 to 700,000. The documents on Jasenovac have been destroyed and only a very small number of prisoners survived. But there is proof, for example, that 17,000 Jews 'disappeared' there. Regardless of the numbers, the fact remains that Jasenovac is the most infamous place in the history of the Croatian people – our own, local, home-made little Auschwitz – and that Dinko Šakić was its commander.

After the war, Šakić was declared a war criminal *in absentia* by a Yugoslav court, but he was never extradited. According to his own account, after fleeing to Austria he spent a couple of months there to help Pavelić escape to Italy, and then he himself left for Argentina, where he lived happily ever after. Most of his life there he spent as a peaceful citizen, running a restaurant with friends. Now he occupies himself by writing his memoirs, in the hope of correcting history.

We actually meet this man, a war criminal, in the lobby of the Hotel Alvear in Buenos Aires, almost exactly fifty years after he left Zagreb. A Croatian journalist is interviewing him for her newspaper. She is a well-known journalist, and as his pet, she is part of President Tudjman's entourage on his first official visit to Argentina.

Now, we all have a certain idea of what a criminal should look like, especially a war criminal. We imagine his weird, if not mean look, detectable by carefully studying the expression on his face, or his eyes, for example. We look for something in his appearance that will disclose his criminal mind. We believe that everything would be much easier if we could actually see that someone is evil. But history demonstrates time and again, that such a thing is not to be detected in someone's appearance. Take Adolf Eichmann, that small, ordinary-looking man, and what Hannah Arendt wrote about him: 'The evil is banal.' I repeated her words to myself as I looked at the latest photo of Mr Šakić, published alongside the interview. Today he is a man of seventy-four and he wears a civilian suit. He looks more like a well-preserved retired bank clerk than an ex-officer or a war criminal. The journalist even writes how he and his wife look a bit lonely and lost in the lobby of the hotel; she claims that it is evident that 'they have many enemies, or, at least, people who don't share their opinions'. She muses that 'they are people without a homeland'. You can tell that she has a certain understanding, even sympathy for them.

I know how it feels to meet someone like Šakić. Unless the person is very unpleasant to you (which usually he is not, quite the contrary), you tend to forget what you know of him – that he is a child molester, a murderer, a sadist, or a criminal. You look at the face in front of you, and you see that he is nervous, or lonely, or sweating – or charming, or entertaining. What you tend to see is simply another human being. Somehow, personal contact softens you, and all of a sudden, you catch yourself thinking: it is not possible that this man has done it, just look at him. What an innocent smile he has! If I had been in that Croatian journalist's shoes, perhaps I would have tried to concentrate on his hands, hands that had actually killed people. We know that on 10 May 1944: 'There was a deadly silence. When five minutes passed and nobody stepped out, [Šakić] got furious and shot the first two prisoners in the row.' And according to this eyewitness account, that of a survivor of Jasenovac, in the next couple of days Šakić himself personally executed two more prisoners.

I can imagine his hand as it pulls out a revolver, then points it at the prisoner's head. He must have felt the soothing, cool metal against his sweaty, wet palm – or was his palm not even sweating? One bullet, then another. Was it easy to do it? Was it a quick job, or did the prisoner make it unpleasant by his cries? Was there only a little blood, or did the blood splash on to his impeccable uniform? What did Mr Šakić feel at that particular moment, when he was master of life and death? Was it a feeling of power, of satisfaction, of relief, or of nothing at all? All these questions were not, but could and should have been asked. To what he is asked, Mr Šakić answers that he 'was doing his job, and that Jasenovac was, to be sure, not a sanatorium, but not a torture ground either, as the Serbs present it'.

Then what was his job, if not that of a murderer, an executioner? The journalist says: 'Have you been an executioner, Mr Šakić?' We know that she asked that, because there is a question-mark at the end of the sentence. As if this were a real question; as if she were interested in the response. It sounds like a joke, because you expect nothing but his denial; indeed, you are prepared for it already by the tone of the interview. 'No, of course not,' he says, perhaps drumming his fingers on the table in boredom. As an officer of the NDH, he was only fulfilling his duty towards his homeland. In response to such questions, he would not say anything else, nor would he admit his guilt. But does that change the name or the character of the acts he committed in Jasenovac, and in this particular instance? Obviously, he thinks that it does, that what he did was fully justified. If anything, Mr Šakić is extremely candid and sincere about his feelings and his past in general. So much so that the journalist admits, not without admiration, that 'he has remained totally faithful to his ideas'.

But what does it really mean, that this war criminal, a murderer and a political loser, has remained devoted to his ideas, even to this day? That he is proud of what he did and that he would do it again? With regard to that, the reporter does actually ask him one good question. She asks Mr Šakić if he is ashamed in front of his children. 'No,' he says, 'I am not ashamed. I am proud. And they are proud of me . . . I would do it again.' But the journalist does not press him further; she is cautious and does not insist on details.

I almost understand her difficult position. It would be extremely discourteous to this nice old gentleman who has politely agreed to give her an interview to bother him with details. He could have refused to be interviewed in the first place. Then, there would not have been a scoop for her. Imagine if she had started insisting on some gruesome detail, like this one, described by the same former prisoner as before: 'There were ten of them altogether. An Ustashe soldier put a bullet into the head of each of them. One prisoner did not die immediately, so he was shot again. But even so, he still showed signs of life. Then the Ustashe soldier took out a knife, slit the prisoner's throat, filled his own hand with the prisoner's blood and drank it in front of us, the other prisoners – perhaps in order to gain the strength of the slaughtered man.'

What would have happened if she had quoted this to Mr Šakić? What was she afraid of? That he would start shouting at her, insulting her, perhaps even threatening her – or just that he would dismiss the accusation with an elegant movement of his hand? For whatever reason, she decides that there is no need to provoke him any further. Besides, she is convinced that her questions are provocative enough for people who understand; she is not a police interrogator. And all these stories, even if true, might have been only isolated incidents. Such cruelty happens in all wars, all armies commit them – look at the Bosnian war now.

This is what I imagine she thinks while she sits there, facing that war criminal, giving him a chance to defend himself – because this is exactly what she does. I have only one doubt: it is not clear to me if she herself knows what this grey-haired gentleman is talking about. Has she herself ever read a single fact, or the testimony of a single witness from Jasenovac, before she lets him go just like that, with his apologia for mass crimes committed by the fascist regime of the NDH, and by himself? Perhaps – just perhaps, although its hard to believe – she shares his opinion that 'there was no mass liquidation in Jasenovac. If you take into account how long the camp was there, and its population, and that deaths were natural and normal, there were always about 3,000 prisoners in the camp.'

The journalist could not get Mr Šakić to confess his guilt, that is obvious. But she could have confronted him with witnesses, descriptions, documents, for the sake of trying, for the sake of balance, for the sake of truth. When Mr Šakić says, 'We were human towards the prisoners . . .

[Jasenovac] was an institution based on the law and those guilty of destroying and undermining the Croatian state, those dangerous to public peace and order, were sent to it,' the journalist should perhaps have asked him, how it was that women and children were considered dangerous to the state and executed en masse too? Or perhaps she should have read the account of another eyewitness to him: 'In front of a brick factory, beside an old electric plant, there lay corpses of those who had been thrown from the upper floor of the factory . . . A weak-looking prisoner ran by me in deadly fear, followed by a tall Ustashe with a big iron bar. "You can't escape from me," the Ustashe shouted. Luckily, he did not see me. A few steps away from me, an old man cried: "Let me only pray to God first!" But he fell down immediately. His skull was crushed.'

Instead she let Mr Šakić tell his story, defending himself, justifying his crimes and crimes of the NDH government, just as if he were merely another witness of those times. Then she let him go. Perhaps this is not what she actually intended. Perhaps she imagined the interview differently, prepared all the right tough questions for him the night before, put them down on the piece of paper that is in front of her now. But while she sips her drink with Mr Šakić in the early evening, suddenly the questions she meant to ask evaporate in the thin air of the air-conditioned lobby, in the pleasant murmur of people around them. His wife is also sitting here – can one, should one, embarrass a man in front of his wife? She is not to blame, she has done nothing, and she doesn't know much about her husband's or her brother's 'jobs', about their duty towards the homeland and how they fulfilled it. It all happened so long ago – fifty years have passed. Fifty years! Maybe the journalist makes an effort, but she is weakened by the whole atmosphere, already too intimate.

However, she decides to make one more attempt to reach his conscience, so she asks him if he sleeps well. This happens halfway through the interview. It is meant to be a difficult, even an unkind question, but in the context it sounds naïve, benign, helpless. 'I sleep like a baby,' he says, almost laughing into her face. Like a baby, that is exactly what he says. Could the opposite be true? Might he have said 'I have bad dreams; I dream about the expressions on the prisoners' faces as they fall to the ground; I dream that someone is shooting at me, that I am a prisoner; I see blown-up corpses floating in the river'? No, no way. After all he had said, I, as a reader, can tell that he indeed sleeps well, without remorse, without regret.

This should have been both the moral and dramatic culmination of the interview, but the journalist doesn't realise it. So she goes on with her pale, politely formulated questions, as if her previous question and his answer have no consequence at all, no echo, no meaning. And they don't, because they are lost in what follows, the words they exchange which are just words, light, empty words, flying between them like white butterflies.

There should have been no more questions after that one, no more dialogue. Then, perhaps, the reader would have had time to take a good look at these words and visualise Mr Šakić, as if in a movie, as he prepares himself for his perfectly innocent baby sleep. He puts on his pyjamas, he brushes his teeth, he looks at his reflection in the bathroom mirror and sees nothing that worries him. In bed, he crosses himself for the sake of his soul, because he still believes he has one. By now, a reader would understand that this old man lost his soul a long, long time ago.

To grasp Mr Šakić's answers, or rather his state of mind, is not difficult. Presumably, he has not had many chances to speak publicly, especially not to the Croatian press, which is the only one he cares about (and the only one that cares about interviewing him). So this is his unique opportunity to 'set the record straight' and to clear his name. It comes as no surprise that he sees himself as a dutiful officer working in the interests of the Croatian state, even if it was a fascist state, even if he did sign orders for mass exterminations and did himself participate in them. We have heard that answer before. It is Mr Šakić's only possible justification. He is not bothered by the fact that fascism has been the most horrifying period in the history of mankind. No, he defends it. Do people ever learn? No, not people like this.

Mr Šakić, the commander of one concentration camp, a place of mass extermination, is a poor man because he is imprisoned in the logic of the justification of his crime. As a human being, he deserves pity – though not forgiveness – for he cannot break out of this circle. His whole life has been a defeat. He would not have been able to get away from his past even if he had wanted to, and this, in a way, is his punishment. If someone wants to listen to what he has to say, of course he will say it. But why does this journalist want to help him to wash his hands? This seems to be her problem, but it is not: it is a problem for all of us.

This interview was published in February 1995, almost on the exact day of the solemn celebration of the fiftieth anniversary of the victory over fascism in Auschwitz. People in Croatia were in the unique position of being able to read an interview with the commander of Jasenovac, in which he praised the concentration camp, at the same time as members of the Croatian government were at Auschwitz, paying tribute to the victims. No such tribute was paid to the victims of Jasenovac. There could have been no ceremony at Jasenovac itself, because it was part of the territory occupied by the Serbs at that time, but there was not even an official remembrance of the victims of Jasenovac in Zagreb, the Croatian capital. Why not? As Dinko Šakić himself explained: 'If the NDH had not existed during the war years, 30 May 1990 would never have happened [the day when the new Croatian state was established, now a national holiday]. *NDH was the foundation on which today's Croatia is built.*'

If he is telling the truth, then today's Croatia is a continuation of the fascist NDH. And no one from the government has denied it. Mr Šakić says this because he is well aware that no one is going to dispute it; that indeed, the government is bringing back the memory of 1941–45. It can be seen in the official revision of history, by the rehabilitation of the Ustashe, in the textbooks, in street names, in language, in celebrating writers and heroes and rewarding others from that period – and, finally, in promoting the *Blut und Boden* ideology. There was no need for an official reaction to this interview. No statement was issued by any single state institution – not by the Academy of Sciences, the Institute for Contemporary History, the Bar Association, human rights groups, opposition parties, nor by any cultural or professional institution, for that matter. Their excuse might have been that this interview was not published in the state-controlled press, but it did not seem as if they were looking for an excuse at all. None of them, except for a few solitary intellectuals and one single newspaper, reacted to Mr Šakić's two key statements: that there were no mass executions in Jasenovac, and that the new Croatian state is a continuation of the fascist NDH. Perhaps no one felt the need to react.

This is the most disturbing thing about the whole story.

Can you imagine, in today's Germany, an interview with Heinrich Himmler being published in which he said: 'I am proud, I would do it again, there is nothing to be ashamed of, there were no mass exterminations'? And this is the only angle from which I think we can look at Mr Šakić's words and the reaction to them in Croatia.

The distinguished-looking war criminal also openly announced his intention to visit his homeland next year. And why not? It doesn't look as if he is in any danger of being imprisoned there. It is more likely that he will be welcomed by members of the government. However, I am positive that this will take the form of a discreet dinner at the President's private residence, rather than a rolling out of the red carpet in public. It is a pity, because it would make a nice third photograph for this sad and shameful collection: one communist general and one fascist commander, an idyllic vision of national reconciliation in today's Croatia.

Who's Afraid of Tito's Wife?

In the early spring of 1994 I was sitting in a restaurant in Tirana with Ilir Hoxha, the elder son of the late Albanian communist dictator Enver Hoxha. That evening, when I had seen Ilir for the first time in the lobby of the Hotel Dajti, tall and bold, he looked like the spitting image of his father. I was not the only one to notice the extraordinary similarity between them. While we walked down the street people greeted him, shook hands with him and asked him how he was. 'How am I?' He waved his hand, lamenting: 'The new government took away the apartment where I lived with my family and moved us into an empty factory storehouse at the periphery. Neither I nor my wife has a job and we are denied passports.'

This complaint was the reason for our meeting. Ilir Hoxha wanted to present his case and to attract the interest of international human rights organisations. His mother, Nexhmia Hoxha, had been tried and sent to prison, but no charges were brought against her two sons and her daughter. Nevertheless, they have been denied their rights as citizens without explanation. What a paradox that Ilir Hoxha should be calling upon human rights organisations, I thought, as he explained in detail all the troubles that had befallen him since the democratic changes swept over his country. Ilir Hoxha, whose father was one of the most notorious dictators in Eastern Europe. It was out of the question that Ilir himself might not have known about the forced-labour camps, the political prisoners and the 'enemies' of the state who disappeared without trace. Even two of his own childhood friends, who grew up with Ilir in the block of villas for the communist party *nomenklatura* – the two sons of the prime minister, Mehmet Shehu, ended up in prison after their father allegedly committed suicide in 1981. Yet this same Ilir now dared to call upon a state ruled by law to respect his citizen's and human rights. And as a citizen of the democratic Albania, not charged with any crime, he had a perfect right to do so – unfortunately, to no avail. I heard that he did not get a passport, and that some months later he was placed under house arrest because of an interview in which he allegedly offended the government.

In other ex-communist countries there were no similar scandals. The last communist rulers were either killed (like Nicolae and Elena Ceauşescu) or they died (like Erich Honecker) or, if they are still alive, they live quietly (like Todor Zhivkov), and this goes for their children as well. Monika Jaruzelska is working as a journalist for the magazine *Tvoj Stil*. A granddaughter of Zhivkov runs a boutique and, according to her, supports herself and her grandfather. Even Nicu Ceauşescu, son of the Romanian dictator, was released from prison a long time ago and now is in business. The new democratic governments are aware that they can't use communist methods – except in Albania and Serbia, that is.

Since her husband's death, Tito's wife, Jovanka Broz, has lived in a villa in Dedinje surrounded by bodyguards. With their permission, she goes out on rare occasions. She does not own the villa, but she does not pay rent for it, either. How could she, when she does not even get her husband's pension? Jovanka Broz enjoys Serbia's state 'charity', although it is forced upon her. She does not possess an identity card or a passport, so she cannot leave the country. After years of such a life she has at least managed to get clothes and private things for everyday use. In the beginning, she did not even have her own dresses.

This kind of state maintenance is usually called imprisonment, or at least house arrest. But Jovanka Broz has never been put on trial and sentenced, or even charged with anything. She has simply been deprived of her citizen's rights. 'Nothing has changed for me in the last fifteen years,' she said in a recent interview with a foreign newspaper. And indeed, the Serbian government has not changed, either. Converted communists are still ruling the country and her situation – a typical example of the communist way of dealing with the 'enemy within' – is proof of that. In a state ruled by law, she would either be sentenced to jail or house arrest, or enjoy the same rights as the other citizens of that state. Indeed, if the rumours about her once having plotted against the great dictator Tito are to be believed, she should be being celebrated as a heroine in today's Serbia.

But instead of representing change, the case of Tito's wife is a symptom of something else: the fear of facing the past. If the past is not turned into a myth that people in power can easily manipulate for their own purposes, then it must be forgotten, erased, destroyed – or arrested. Witnesses should not be allowed to speak, for that could be dangerous. Jovanka Broz is an important witness to history, and no doubt she has information that could cause problems to those in power, although, judging by the experience of other ex-communist countries, she would probably be too frightened to talk. But the people in power obviously prefer to keep her in isolation and to strip her of all her rights to prevent her from telling, just in case. She does not have children to fight for her and the international human rights organisations have too much to cope with in the Balkans already. The image of Serbia in the rest of the world is so bad that the case of Jovanka Broz can hardly make it worse. It seems that everybody in Serbia is trying their best to forget her, just as they are trying hard to forget the whole of the recent past.

In the Balkans, history seems to be merely raw material to be recycled to produce daily myths. It is rewritten over and over again – indeed, in the last decade by the very same people. It is an enemy that must be dealt with in a radical, bloody way, even if it means destroying your own little life, your own little biography and your own past.

One can see that for those in power this is a necessity, if they want to retain that power. But ordinary people thereby make themselves an easy object of manipulation by governments. It means that all of us are hiding some kind of Jovanka Broz, an unwanted witness locked up in the dark cell of our conscience.

An Unforgettable Meeting

On 7 August 1995, the London *Times* published a map showing the division of Bosnia between Croatia and Serbia, drawn by the Croatian President on the back of a menu (or maybe a napkin) during a banquet held in London to celebrate the fiftieth anniversary of the end of the Second World War. And while the whole world wondered how he could have committed such a *faux pas* as to reveal the plans he was to realise only two months later by taking back Krajina, I can easily imagine how it happened.

Relaxed and happy to have been invited to such an important event (he had been a bit afraid he might not be, because of Croatia's reputation in the Western world for having rehabilitated Pavelić's wartime fascist regime) President Tudjman chats with the world's politicians. This makes him feel good, because it confirms that he is one of them. The company of mighty men like Köhl, Mitterrand, Major and Hurd suits him perfectly. Looking around, he can see that he is no worse than them, perhaps even better. He is dressed in an expensive, tailor-made suit. Tall, tanned, and slim from playing tennis, with thick grey hair, he does not look his age. He is seventy-three years old, but one would put him at perhaps sixty-five. His teeth are perfect and he speaks English – a sort of English, as the Brits probably say behind his back. Moreover, he is not only the President of one of the newly independent European states, but also an historian and an intellectual, which makes him more distinguished than many of his fellow guests at this solemn gathering.

President Tudjman takes another look at the dining room of the Guildhall. The food has been surprisingly good, considering that this is England. He loved the roast beef and veal with that yellow sauce; he can feel the Dom Perignon running pleasantly through his veins. Yes, he is pleased with himself, he feels important, and why shouldn't he? He has achieved so much in only five years; in fact, he can't think of anyone but himself who has come as far. It has been a long road from his position as a retired general and dissident historian to becoming the leader of the biggest opposition party, and ultimately the first elected President of the new Croatian republic. And almost all of that he has achieved while fighting a war against Serbian aggressors which has crippled his country. To tell the truth, there was another war which he led against Bosnia, although he would prefer to forget this second one. In fact, he has forgotten it, but the world has not.

Ah, the world, thinks Tudjman, it remembers what it wants and forgets what it wants, too. Look at its best statesmen and politicians, drinking and gossiping, plotting and courting each other. If Tudjman has learned anything in the last few years, it is that one should not pay too much attention to the world. Definitely not. One should mind one's own business. Paradoxically, Tudjman learned this lesson from his enemy, Slobodan Milosevic. Soon enough I'll surprise them all, I'll show the world who I am, he thinks, taking another glass of champagne from a silver tray.

Then Paddy Ashdown approaches him. Tudjman would have preferred to have been sought out by Prime Minister John Major rather than by some minor liberal–democratic leader. But he is in a good mood today and does not mind too much. To him, it is important that he is important. So when Ashdown asks him to explain to him what will happen in Bosnia (because what else would Ashdown, or anyone else, ask?), Tudjman sees it as quite normal to reveal to the Englishman exactly what was going to happen. The question could have come from a Serbian spy, a journalist, or the Queen herself – it would not have mattered. He is always eager to explain things to people, simply because he is convinced that he knows best. Essentially, he is the preacher of his own gospel, and as such, he is of course compelled to enlighten everyone. Naturally, he can't stand interruptions or corrections, not to mention any opposing view. This can throw him off balance, and when he loses his temper – well, it is better not to be around. At least, this is what his close collaborators say about him. So, in answer to Ashdown's question, Tudjman grabs a menu from the table and, taking out his gold fountain pen, a gift from some rich Croat living in Chicago (or Munich, or Toronto), he begins to draw a map.

Did Ashdown at that point expect the revelation of a secret plan? Could he have expected anything more than a polite, general response to his question? Certainly not. Let's imagine, for the fun of it, that on a similar occasion in May 1945, someone asked President Roosevelt what he intended to do with Japan, and he replied: 'Well, I will bomb Hiroshima and Nagasaki in exactly three months from now with my new secret weapon, an atomic bomb.' True, Tudjman is not Roosevelt, and taking back the Krajina region and dividing Bosnia between himself and Milošević is not quite the same thing as dropping an atomic bomb, but the fact remains that no president would do such a thing as to draw a map of his plans for any passerby.

As he bends over the table, Tudjman has a concentrated, serious expression on his face, like a general before a decisive battle. This habit is a legacy of the early days, when he was Tito's youngest general, and had to impress people with his stern face rather than with age and experience. He was a kind of communist commissar, in charge of propaganda. Knowing that much about Tudjman, Ashdown must have wondered for a moment how it was possible for an ardent communist to transform himself into a nationalist zealot. But while he watches Tudjman drawing, Ashdown observes his stiff posture, the rigidity of his body that not even Dom Perignon can soften. There is nothing spontaneous about this man; nothing pleasant, either. Looking at him, it perhaps occurs to Ashdown that precisely this combination, the rigidity of both Tudjman's body and his mind, poisoned with ideology at an early age, is the answer to the riddle of his transformation: there in fact was no transformation at all. Ideas have changed, from Marxism to nationalism, but what remains is his love of ideology itself. This makes him a lousy historian, since he cares less about science than he does about propagating certain ideas. On the other hand, this is what makes him a leader – albeit a dangerous, dictatorial type of leader who never hesitates or has doubts about what is the right thing to do. He strongly believes in Croatian nationalism, but more than anything else, he believes in himself.

How strange that this man, who in his books disputed

the number of Jews killed during the holocaust in Europe, and the number of people killed in the Croatian concentration camp at Jasenovac, was present at the opening of the Holocaust Museum in Washington, Ashdown perhaps asks himself. Following the quick movements of Tudjman's elegant hand and gold pen, Ashdown might be thinking about how Tudjman, with no shame at all, appointed his son as deputy chief of military intelligence, as if running a state was the same as running a family business. Or how his other son, as well as his daughter, also got rich through being related to him, and how even his young grandson became a bank owner. One must wonder how it is possible to do all this without any political consequences if Croatia is not a sort of European banana republic.

Now Tudjman, in his stammering English, starts to explain to Ashdown how he is going to gain control of Krajina, while Tuzla, Goražde and Eastern Slavonia will remain Serbian. Ashdown is becoming really interested in what Tudjman is saying, for he is no longer explaining what has happened, but what will happen in that frightening part of the world. But somehow, being a politician himself, surely he cannot believe this. Why would Tudjman tell him what he really intends to do? He can't be that crazy, that arrogant, that self-assured in his power. Not knowing Tudjman well, he probably thinks that Tudjman is speculating, toying with the idea of taking Krajina and dividing Bosnia. Speculations and wishful thinking, he perhaps mutters to himself, deciding not to pay attention to Tudjman's words. What would be the rational explanation for this man to tell him exactly what he plans to do?

Ashdown takes another look at Tudjman's face. His expression – the frown and the thin, tight lips – has not changed. He looks like an offended muppet. There is something repulsive about his grimace, as if he were wearing a mask that he can't remove, a mask that has turned into his real face. People compare him to Tito, but he has no sense of humour, he is not as easy-going as that old maverick and he has no elegance or *savoir-faire*.

By now, Ashdown must have noticed two things about Tudjman's face, because everybody notices them straight away. First, he is not able to look you in the eye. His eyes slide around like quicksilver. He gives the impression that he is looking at nothing, listening to his own voice, as if the identity of the listener is utterly unimportant. He does not hold conversations, he just talks. This can be best seen on television. He never looks into the camera. A modern politician should be aware – and if he is not, someone should discreetly point it out to him – that he has to look straight into the camera, pretending that he is making eye contact with the viewer. He has to create a personal relationship with the viewer, to convince him, to seduce him, to conquer his vote. But Tudjman ignores the camera; for him it does not matter. In doing so, he reveals that he is an old-school politician, used to speaking in front of masses of people, in squares or in huge halls designed for Communist Party congresses. His eyes do not matter there, for no one can see them. What matters is the tone of his voice, his pose, his gestures.

The other awkward feature of Tudjman's face is that smile of his. It is not really even a smile, but a kind of painful cramp that makes him look sarcastic, even sardonic, especially when he tries to laugh. What comes out is a smirk. It is not easy for anybody to live with this kind of face, much less so for a politician, but Tudjman manages quite well. In spite of possessing characteristics that would easily disqualify him in a real race for voters in a Western country, he has had astonishing success as a leader in his country. Post-communist countries seem to prefer father figures to democratic representatives, and he fits very well into this pattern.

Tudjman has now finished his map, and in a matter-of-fact voice he explains to Ashdown that he has the tacit approval of Milošević for his plan to take over Krajina and to incorporate within it parts of Bosnia. Ashdown must be even more astonished that Tudjman is not even trying to lie about, or even hide, his relations with Milošević or Izetbegović, whom he, with open contempt, calls a Muslim fundamentalist. Clearly, Tudjman is no bureaucrat or diplomat. He is too convinced of his historical mission to bother with such things. Once an American diplomat told him, quite ironically: 'Mr President, I am convinced that you have an historical mission for your nation.' With tears in his eyes, Tudjman turned to his wife. 'Listen, Ankica, to what Ambassador X is saying!'

Who does he really think he is? Churchill, Roosevelt, Stalin? perhaps Ashdown asks himself as he looks at this strange man in front of him. While Ashdown is no doubt amazed that any politician should commit such a terrible error, it may be that he has not reckoned with Tudjman's main characteristic: his vanity. Tudjman is not a politician. A politician would never do this, because it would spell the end for him. But what is a man supposed to think of himself when the president of the Croatian parliament says that he is the first Croat leader to appear for 900 years? No wonder Tudjman has acquired a kind of Messiah complex: he has been chosen by Providence to lead his nation out of communist–Serbian slavery. Probably, every night before he goes to sleep he already sees a statue of himself in the main square in Zagreb. His love for historical perspectives is well known: he always expresses himself in centuries, if not millennia – a 1,000-year old Croatian dream of independence; the Maslenica Bridge liberated for the coming 1,000 years – and he can easily visualise himself as part of the millennium scheme of things. And while he reveals his future plans to a perfect stranger, Tudjman is only acting normally, that is, in accordance with his own image of himself.

Is he not even afraid that this drawing on the back of a menu will become known to his countrymen and provoke outrage against him? One doubts that the thought ever came to his mind. In his recollections of the collapse of Yugoslavia, Warren Zimmermann, the last American ambassador to Yugoslavia, describes how he once had breakfast with Tudjman, that 'inflexible schoolteacher', as he aptly encapsulates a part of Tudjman's character. Out of the blue, Tudjman appointed two of his aides who accompanied him to the meeting to very high posts. On the spot, just like that – no consultations with the Prime Minister, no parliamentary decision. Imperial behaviour indeed. In his historical, imperial and Messianic perspective, cemented by a strong police and even stronger army, a few voices of protest will make no difference, not to mention bring about change.

Everyone has noticed his love for uniforms trimmed with gold, for gold chains, crosses, decorations and medals, newly invented by a team of designers creating the new national symbolism. He obviously feels good dressed in a white marshal's uniform with all nine of the decorations that he more or less awarded himself pinned to his chest. However, all he has achieved is to become a living imitation of people he has read about and admires. This pathetic posturing makes him look like a caricature of some South American dictator. Who but Tudjman is doing this in

Europe today? That inclination for theatrics and kitsch reveals not only the bad taste of a typical representative of the province, but also the kind of cruel cynicism of an Oriental despot. Refugees, poverty, war, bloodshed – nothing prevents Tudjman from exhibiting his uniforms, his decorations, his power and his endless ambitions.

It seems as if all this third-rate politician is missing now is a crown and a sceptre. There are rumours in Croatia that he will proclaim himself Ban – a kind of duke. Who will stop him, if he decides to do this? After all, he invented the stage, he wrote the script and he has cast himself in the leading role of this historical play about independence. What is to prevent him from becoming king of this fictional world?

Perhaps the saddest thing to see is Tudjman's enormous greed for life. One has the feeling that he is swallowing it in big gulps. A latecomer to power, he is so hungry for everything that power can bring – glory, money, obedience, importance – that he can't stop stuffing himself with it. Aware that he has about ten years at most to taste it all, he has no inclination to wait. He just grabs what he can while he can.

Poor country, Ashdown must think as Tudjman gives him a severe look, incoherent, though his twisted grimace is evidently a clue that it is a smile. Eager to let him know that he finally understands everything, Ashdown takes the menu with the map on it and pretends to study it. At that moment, someone approaches Tudjman, and Ashdown walks away with a map in his pocket, a weird souvenir of this unforgettable meeting with the Croatian President.

Three months later, he finds it again, only to realise, to his utter astonishment, that what Tudjman disclosed to him was indeed the truth.

Still Stuck in the Mud

When I look through the window of the bedroom, I see nothing. The apartment is situated on the fourth floor of a building in northern Stockholm and the bedroom overlooks a yard. There is the grey façade of the neighbouring house, small lamps lit in the windows, TV screen flickering and the shadows of people moving in the warm bellies of their flats. And when I look downwards, there is a yard.

Ever since I first set my eyes on that yard I did not like it. For no particular reason, except that it seemed unpleasant, hostile even, to me. It took me some time to understand why. The yard is empty. The cemented area of about 30 by 20 metres is unbearably clean and neat. There is not a single piece of paper to be seen there, a clothes peg that has fallen from a balcony, or a forgotten toy. Just a few bicycles, parked in an orderly way in a bicycle rack. No activity, no life, no voices of children playing with a ball after school, not even in the summer. I suspect that here, in Sweden, no one knows any longer what such a yard is for. Its emptiness is a definite sign of the highly urbanised life in this city.

For generations now, people here haven't needed to turn their yards into extensions of their apartments, to store their supplies of food there, to carry out small repairs, clean their carpets, hang clothes to dry, leave their kids to play, or simply to chat and gossip with neighbours. Living in a modern Western city provides easy access to all the necessary services, but also entails respecting written and unwritten laws of privacy. In a city, you can choose with whom you want to share your space and interests, be it in the office, in a restaurant, or at the gym. In a village, you don't have such a choice, because you depend on each other too much, as you also do in the not entirely urbanised cities of Eastern Europe. This is why the common space, such as the yards, looks different in Western cities.

When I think of yards, another picture surfaces in my mind. It is Saturday. A man is washing his car, dressed in a blue nylon sweatsuit; another man, perhaps a mechanic, is repairing a machine, probably to make some extra money; a woman is hanging out clothes to dry; children are playing; several elderly people are just sitting watching, while a cat lazily strolls between them all. Through open windows you can hear voices shouting, a cartoon playing on TV, folk music, a vacuum cleaner. There is a smell of beef soup, of pancakes and baked potatoes. You immediately understand that this yard is vital breathing space for people who live in flats which are too small and too crowded, often with three generations together under the same roof. It is a space where you can engage in all kinds of different activities: moonlighting, playing, quarrelling. Yet a clean yard like this one in Stockholm is the ideal of urban society: it is our ideal too, I suppose.

For an outsider, say a Swede, this Eastern European Saturday scene would perhaps give the impression that we are living too close to each other, that our lives are too transparent. It would remind him of life in a small, tightly knit community bound to live together. He would be perfectly right. Compared to Stockholm, or any such city, our urban life is different. It is much closer to life in the countryside. Cities in Eastern Europe, especially in the Balkans, still have retained some of the flavour of the village, both in the appearance and habits of their inhabitants.

In fact, if you take a closer look at such a city, you are compelled to ask yourself: where does the village end and the city begin? Perhaps all cities, even those in Western Europe, crumble at the edges, gradually becoming poorer and more dilapidated, in a way dissolving into their surrounding area. The dividing line between rural and urban, is simply hard to define here. I know where the city of Stockholm ends, because I can see that from my window, too: my friend lives in the last block of the city houses, in a yellow five-storey apartment building, where in the old times there was a real border, a customs house. Then there is a thick, dark wood and beyond that the suburbs, which are almost hidden by it. There are no family houses or building sites, as I am used to.

This sight of the city's abrupt end (or beginning) fascinates me, because of its unfamiliarity. The general rule in my part of the world is: the closer you are to the periphery, the less asphalt and cement there will be in the yards and on the streets; the more junk, construction sites and more poverty. The houses get smaller and shabbier, as if hammered into the soil, crouching between huge half-finished apartment blocks growing up in the middle of nowhere.

So I don't quite know where Zagreb, or Warsaw, say,

end. When I was invited to a friend's apartment in a new part of Warsaw, I ended up somewhere that could just as well have been Belgrade or Sofia. The settlement looked like a big dormitory, a kind of honeycomb for people, where streets were not yet asphalted and still had no names. There were no streetlights, no shops and no signs of civilisation except for parked cars. When I asked my friend when they had moved in, she told me that they had lived for three years on that building site, surrounded by cranes and bulldozers, because there is no money to finish the work.

The peripheries of our cities usually develop in all directions in a strange way, like a sick organism, an unconnected, torn-apart tissue: ghostly skyscrapers on the horizon, heaps of building debris, heavy industry plant with family houses caught in between, garbage deposits, huts, farms, small patches of vegetable gardens and entire villages swallowed up a long time ago, connected if you are lucky by muddy roads ending somewhere in the fields.

The further you move away from the centre of such a city, the more picturesque its yards become. In such a yard at the periphery you'll find a rusty barrel full of rainwater for the vegetables in the garden, because running water is expensive; a car wreck already half covered by grass; tyres; pieces of old furniture and flowerpots – all wedged between strange-looking but important wooden huts of various sizes. These are improvised storerooms, usually covered with tar paper, where food supplies are kept through the winter: sacks of potatoes and cabbage, apples, carrots and onions. Because people are less confined by the discipline of the city, they build a bit here and there, according to their needs. Building without a permit is illegal, of course, but building inspectors from the town hall don't come here very often. Consequently there are hundreds of bulging houses with additional rooms tacked on at the back, built overnight to accommodate a growing family, garages made out of metal sheets, shelters for wooden logs, work sheds, boxes for rabbits and hen houses. Gradually, almost imperceptibly, these junkyards give way to potato fields and pigsties and stables and suddenly, without ever really having left the city, we find ourselves in the country. The presence of animals – the stench from the hens, chickens, rabbits, goats, pigs (especially pigs) should perhaps be considered the real border.

You might associate mud with rural areas, but in Eastern European cities it returns to haunt you, the ghost of your peasant origins. I remember that it rained early that morning in Bucharest, and as I walked towards the old marketplace in the centre, I thought I'd never get there. The streets were covered with mud and were so slippery that it was dangerous to walk there. It appeared under the asphalt, through holes and cracks – brownish, sticky, greasy, just like shit. I tried to watch my step, jumping over puddles, but there was no way of escaping the mud. It stuck to the soles of my shoes, splashing high up to my knees. As I approached the market, I felt as if I were plunged into some kind of a primordial soup, dragged back to the origins of life, dissolving into basic elements, so primeval did that mud look to me, so omnipresent, so inevitable.

And after every fall of rain or snow it comes back again. The mud never disappears from our streets. Why, I wondered that morning, do I see it everywhere? Between the streetcar tracks in Prague, in the gutters, gushing out from the access points to the street drains in Zagreb, in downtown Sofia, in Bratislava. It is always there, under our feet. When the rain stops, the mud dries up and turns into a layer of yellow dust which covers pavements, windows, buildings, cars. You know that it is there, just sleeping under the patched roads and among the cobblestones, waiting for its chance to overtake the city. You are not safe. When the mud comes out, it follows you to your house, up the staircase, into the elevator, right on to the living room carpet.

It seems like a sort of plot: from time to time the soil rises from beneath us, just to remind us where we come from, to tell us that most of us are only the first generation of urban citizens. Our grandparents štill live in the villages, and our parents were born there. But the soil is what we want to forget – the stench, the poverty of Grandma's house, the mud at its threshold, the outdoor toilet, the traces of chicken blood in the yard, the complaints about hard work exchanged over thick soup.

Our ambivalence towards mud is as difficult to get rid of as the mud itself. One of the reasons for this is the way the cities developed. Before the Second World War, Yugoslavia was a peasant country: over 80 per cent of its population lived in rural areas. This was the case in other Eastern European countries, too, although the percentage of peasants varied between typical peasant countries in the Balkans, such as Bulgaria or Romania, and the more industrialised ones in Central Europe, like Czechoslovakia. After the war, however, the new communist governments engaged in the collectivisation of the land and forced industrialisation on a mass scale. Workers were badly needed, so the peasants moved into cities, which rapidly started to grow in order to accommodate all the new-comers, swelling as if they were pregnant. Construction began on a rampant and haphazard scale.

The people building the houses were themselves among

those who had only just arrived in the cities, unskilled or semi-skilled labourers with particular working habits. In order to survive, they kept two jobs, working in the fields as well as in the city. At harvest time they would take a long sick leave. These people were neither experienced in construction, nor particularly motivated. To make matters worse, there were never enough building materials, because of the workers' predilection for stealing cement, sand, bricks, tiles – anything that could be used to improve their own miserable houses or city apartments. They could not get materials any other way because either they were expensive or there were none available at all, so they smuggled them out of the factories and the building sites. The new houses therefore had to be built with insufficient cement and bricks, which not surprisingly resulted in disasters. As soon as such buildings were finished, or even before they were, they started to collapse. The same thing happened to the hastily built streets and roads, which often cracked. They were either patched up or left with holes like wounds, where the mud came out.

It was, nevertheless, considered a great achievement for a family to move from a village hut into a 32 square-metre apartment on the eighth floor of a skyscraper. It was much better than living next to a pigsty and breaking your back digging in a field from dawn to dusk. This whole phenomenon of quick expansion was called 'progress'. Progress reached the villages, too, in the form of asphalted roads and the introduction of electricity. I was barely able to read when my great-grandmother wrote to me with the news that the new roads had finally caught up with her village in the island of Krk. She wrote that with a certain pride, but I remembered the warmth on my bare feet of the small stone-paved streets which led down towards the harbour, and I was not too happy with that aspect of progress. I remember, too, the portly local politicians who, in the sixties, would go to every village after the first kilometre of new road had been built in order to declare it opened by cutting a ribbon and eating a roasted lamb afterwards. At that time, progress was measured in kilometres of asphalt and numbers of electric bulbs.

I can imagine what relief the asphalt must have brought, what it must have meant to be able to walk on the smooth, grey surface in your fine leather shoes without getting them dirty. Everyone who moved from the village into the city, or even those urban people who occasionally visit a village today, must have felt the same way. After filling your car with potatoes and hens, eggs and ham and fruit and Grandma's apple pie, you rush back gratefully to the city, feeling slightly dirty, aware of the strange country odour your clothes have absorbed, the mud sticking stubbornly to your shoes. The city is where you belong, you think, as do millions of first-generation city people.

You would think that being born in the city in the fifties would be enough to qualify you as a fully fledged urban person, but it is not quite that simple. We have a feeling of ambivalence, of hate and love, of contempt for and dependence on the village and its mud. We have never really cut free from our peasant roots, nor could we have done even if we'd wanted to, because we would have starved. Keeping one foot in the village is probably one of the ways in which people in Eastern Europe have been able to survive food rationings and shortages of all kinds. By keeping in close touch with your grandparents, or with more distant relatives in the village from which your family comes, or with friends and acquaintances (there will always be someone there who remembers you!), you can be sure of a supply of potatoes at least. And around Christmastime, when the rural folk slaughter their pigs, there is always enough meat and enough home-made sausages, as well as a good piece of bacon, for you to take some back home with you.

The practical problem with food brought home from the village is, of course, where to put it. In 'wealthy' households you often notice big deep-freeze boxes acquired for that purpose. More often you have to solve the problem by turning your balcony into a kind of storage room. But if this still does not give you enough space, you must go into the yard and build an improvised storehouse there. The yard takes on a different look then, a city too.

So here we are again, back in the yard, adapting the city to our needs, bending it to other rules, taming it to accommodate the habits of its new inhabitants, changing it. You soon forget the Godforsaken village, the relatives there, the neglected graveyard and the odd smell. After all, your life has been changed by the city: you are a sophisticated urban person, you have a car and you walk on asphalt. Except when it rains, when the mud comes out to remind you. There you are, with one foot still stuck in the mud, still a million miles away from that clean, empty yard in Stockholm.

Because the village is a means of survival, even today.

Bosnia, or What Europe Means to Us

It was the best *sarma* I had ever tasted: small, tightly wrapped in sauerkraut and compact. The *sarma* is made of minced meat mixed with chopped onions, some garlic, salt, a whole egg and spices. The Bosnian *sarma* comes without sauce and is served with sour cream instead, which gives it that special, delicious taste. I used to make it myself from time to time, but I would mix rice into the meat and make a sauce of sweet red paprika and tomato puree, the variation of the recipe on the Adriatic coast, where I come from.

As well as the *sarma*, the Sunday lunch table was laid with filled onions called *dolma*; *burek*, a pie of a thin home-made pastry stuffed with meat, and *zeljanica*, another with spinach and cheese; and a plate of tasty grilled meat, *ćevapčići*. In the middle there was a beautiful round loaf of bread, twisted into a plait. You don't cut this with a knife, you just break off pieces and stuff yourself with it until you can hardly breathe. And, of course, to end it all, there was *baklava*, a traditional sweet made with nuts without which no festive Bosnian meal would be complete. Considering the fact that we were in Stockholm, this lunch was even more special, because the Bosnian family who had invited us had had to put a lot of effort into finding all the right ingredients. But they must have known exactly where to get them, because everything was just perfect, as if you were eating in the middle of Sarajevo.

I asked Fatima, the mother who prepared the meal with the help of her twenty-year-old daughter, Amira, what kind of meat she used for the *sarma*. Was it half beef, half pork, as I used? 'Oh, no,' she said, 'I use only beef. It gives the *sarma* a much better taste.' It occurred to me then that the reason she didn't use pork was probably that they were religious Muslims, but I immediately regretted making that assumption. A couple of years ago such a thought would not even have entered my head, but now, after four years of war, even a question about a recipe was no longer innocent. Since then, we have all gradually learned how to think differently, how to divide people into Muslims, Croats and Serbs, even in terms of food. This is what war did to us. It brought us to extreme awareness, extreme sensitivity, because belonging to one nation or another could make the difference between life and death. I was ashamed of having automatically categorised the family. And in any case, I was wrong. Zijo, the father, was drinking brandy – *rakija* – along with the rest of us and there was whisky and wine offered at the table, too. Evidently they were non-religious, though brought up with the influence of the Muslim culture, as are the majority of Bosnian Muslims.

The family – Zijo, Fatima and Amira – had come to Sweden in 1992, soon after the war in Bosnia had started. The Swedish authorities found them a sunny, two-bedroomed apartment in a working-class suburb of

Stockholm. They were also given money with which to furnish it. They had spent some of this on a television set, which was clearly the most important feature of their pleasant living room, if not the centre of their lives. During lunch, the set remained switched on, even if the volume was turned down. The father glanced at it frequently, waiting for the satellite news programme. He watches both the Serbian and Croatian broadcasts. There was a video, too. One of Zijo's activities – and he has little else to do – is to visit his friends, Bosnian refugees in other parts of the city, and exchange or borrow tapes from the 'homeland', whatever that word means to these people nowadays. It doesn't matter if it is a movie, a musical, a show or a news programme, anything will do. They watch them all. They can't live without them; or at least, Zijo can't.

Zijo was a civil servant in his former life. Now, in his mid-fifties, he no longer has a job and cannot provide for his family. Too young to retire, he just doesn't know what to do with himself. In the middle of a conversation he falls silent because he spots something on the television which takes him back into his old world. Or he just drifts away into his own thoughts, sitting there, listening, but not really participating. His body is idle; there is no wood to cut, no way to be useful. It's easier for women, they always have something to do, he says with a shy smile, as if he is at the same time apologising for his patriarchal mentality in this very 'politically correct' country. But he speaks a simple truth. Fatima runs the household, just as she used to do in Bosnia. In fact for her, things are a bit easier now, because she used to work full time and do all the housework. She misses her job a lot, but she has not lost the meaning of her life. She still has to keep her family together, to cook, to take care of the house. She also goes to a Swedish-language class provided free by the state for refugees.

For their daughter, the problems of adapting to a new country are less severe. In four years she has learned the language all by herself and is now working for her high-school degree. Like any person of her age, Amira has plans. She wants to study in Stockholm. In the meantime, she takes on temporary jobs; she goes out with her new friends to a disco, perhaps, and generally doesn't miss Bosnia all that much, except for her old friends. But most of them are no longer there anyway.

Perhaps because of the nature of her daily work, Fatima is more focused on the present. She thinks that the family should stay in Sweden and see what happens after the Dayton Agreement, whether peace in Bosnia will hold. She knows that their daughter has better opportunities for education and getting a good job in Sweden than she would have in insecure Bosnia, and she is prepared to stay until Amira gets her university degree. Zijo does not directly oppose his wife – how could he, when she has valid, rational arguments on her side? But you can tell that he would leave this cosy apartment in an instant to find himself among his own people again. It doesn't mean that he has any illusions about them, that he doesn't ask himself how much they will have changed because of the war. But he would still give up the comfort and security for what he is missing the most, his country, if only he could. You would probably have to start your life from scratch there, I say. He nods. He knows that in order to regain the life he once had back home, he would need to work hard for many years all over again. In Sweden, everything was just given to them. And just like that, says Zijo. He is appreciative, but he can't help asking himself how any society can be affluent enough to afford all that. I sense that he feels he is a burden, and that this cannot be a nice feeling.

The family has a brand-new washing machine in the bathroom, something you don't often see in Swedish households. People usually share two or three washing machines between a whole apartment building. This system works well, except that you have to put yourself on a list about a week in advance to do your laundry, but not knowing about it, the family bought their own machine. It is difficult to be forced to live in another country, to be obliged to change your habits, so they try to stick to what they know when they can. They wash their clothes in their own machine, and they travel about forty-five minutes or more to the market in the centre of town to get all the right ingredients for *dolma* or *zeljanica* or *baklava*. Surrounded by a tidy park, silent neighbours and a strange language, their life is divided between two realities – one here, in Sweden, in Europe; the other back home, in Bosnia.

Zijo shows interest in only a couple of topics: the latest news and the possibilities for peace (which for him equates to when he might be able to go home), and the past, or how did it all happen to us? He has no doubt that it was the political elite, not ordinary people like himself, who started the war. First people were talked into it, next they found it forced upon them, and then it was too late, he says. 'Now I feel like the country I've left – cut into pieces. Some parts of me are still there, some parts are here, but certain parts are lost forever.'

When I ask him what he thinks of Europe he waves his hand dismissively, as if one should not waste too many words on the subject. Only when I insist that he describes his attitude towards Europe, does he start by telling me a story about a wooden house. He saw it recently nearby, a wooden house built in the typical Swedish style. 'I was admiring its simplicity,' he tells me, 'and then I thought that I should take a photograph of that house and send it to my relatives back home. But I did not do it. I changed my mind. Having lived here for some time now, I understand that the house is beautiful to me because I am able to understand its beauty. In Bosnia they would think it was poor. Who, in my part of the world, but very poor people would build a wooden house? People there are proud when they build a two-storey ugly cement block, the bigger the better, so that the neighbours can see that you've made it. There are certain differences between us and Europe, but there are many misunderstandings, too.' Zijo, like many other Bosnians, has seen both faces of Europe, the nice one and the ugly one.

The Bosnians were so painfully naïve. I remember them saying, even when the war had already started, 'Europe will not let us be divided.' Even after the heavy shelling of Sarajevo, and the deaths of tens of thousands of people, the Bosnians still looked towards Europe with hope. 'Europe must do something to stop the killing,' they would say. If you did not know what 'Europe' was, you might well conclude that it was not a continent, but a single entity, a powerful, Godlike being. It took the Bosnians years to realise that Europe was not what they had imagined it to be, and only then after they were let down in the most shameful way. Europe is just a bunch of states with different interests, and the Bosnians had to discover this through their hesitation, indifference and cynicism. Paradoxically, hundreds of thousands of them ended up in European countries as refugees, and it was only then that they were helped.

If peace should have been imposed in the Balkans, the

European countries should have imposed it in the first place, not left it to the Americans. They know the Balkans better. For decades Yugos used to clean their streets and build their cities as *Gastarbeiter*. With a minimum of effort Europeans can distinguish Zagreb from Belgrade or Sarajevo, and Banja Luka from Skopje, and there is a fair chance that some of them might once have even visited Dubrovnik. Yet, the European countries had trouble regarding the Balkans as a part of Europe. At the beginning of the war, for a long time the European states behaved as if it was a problem of semantics.

Zijo, lost in Stockholm, eating *sarma* and watching a television programme from back home, is suffering the consequences of this semantic problem. But the consequence of this problem is tens of thousands of wounded and disabled in Bosnia as well. This should and could have been prevented in the first place. If the war in Bosnia could not have been prevented, it could at least have been stopped long before Dayton and on many occasions. Every time the Serbs were really threatened and became afraid of being bombed, they would withdraw and agree to negotiate. Lives could have been saved, and the exodus of more than 2 million people prevented. Providing that the Dayton agreement is the end of the ordeal, the results of the war in the Balkans will be borders changed by force (according to a European precedent after the Second World War), the acknowledgement of ethnic cleansing and the pushing of the Bosnian Muslims into the hands of fundamentalist Muslims from the Middle East – perhaps an irreversible European mistake.

Nobody should be killed because of his 'wrong' national affiliation or the 'wrong' colour of his eyes. But it is an even bigger tragedy if people are killed because of what they are not. This terrible fate is exactly what has befallen the Bosnians. They were 'ethnically cleansed' at the beginning of the war on the pretext that they were religious Muslims, even fundamentalists. Of course, this was not true, merely a justification for what both the Serbs and the Croats wanted to do: to scare people away from 'their' territory. It is astonishing, however, that the European states, too, behaved as if the Muslims in Bosnia were religious. It should not have been too difficult to look at a few simple facts about the Bosnian Muslims in order to understand the problem. For example, they are not Arabs, but are of Slavic origin; they were given Muslim nationality in the mid-seventies by Tito, in order to maintain the balance between Serbs and Croats in Bosnia. Although their culture, as a result of the Turkish occupation, is Muslim-influenced, the majority do not practise the Muslim religion. For some reason, however – was it fear of the rise of Muslim fundamentalism in Europe, combined with the very convenient theory of the 'ancient hatred' of the peoples in the Balkans? – it was taken as read that the Bosnian Muslims were about to establish a Muslim fundamentalist republic in the heart of Europe. For this purpose, the Balkans suddenly became part of Europe, and this could not be permitted. So the Bosnian Muslims were not helped by the European states, but instead by countries like Iran.

What was their alternative? If you were being killed as Muslim fundamentalists in spite of being a European, non-religious, Slavic people of Muslim nationality, and the only source of help were Muslim countries you would finally be forced to turn Muslim in order to survive. Bosnians made a pact with the Devil, but there was nobody else to make a pact with. After that, Bosnia was probably lost to Europe, as Europe was lost to the Bosnians a long time before.

It seems to me that a part of the tragedy of the Bosnians lies in their belief that Europe is what it is not. Europe did not intervene, it did not save them, because there was no Europe to intervene. They saw a ghost. It was us, the Eastern Europeans, who invented 'Europe', constructed it, dreamed about it, called upon it. This Europe is a myth created by us, not only Bosnians, but other Eastern Europeans, too – unfortunate outsiders, poor relatives, the infantile nations of our continent. Europe was built by those of us living on the edges, because it is only from there that you would have the need to imagine something like 'Europe' to save you from your complexes, insecurities and fears. Because for us, the people from the Balkans, the biggest fear is to be left alone with each other. We have learned better than others what you do to your own brother.

Sitting there at the Sunday lunch with Zijo, Fatima, Amira and their friends, I felt the absurdity of their situation. Why were these people in Stockholm? Was the food they were eating – *sarma, dolma, pita, ćevapčići* – the reason why they had been driven from their own country? The idea seems crazy, I know, but what else is the reason? They didn't look different from me, or from those who had scared them away from their home. We even share the language, the education and history of the last fifty years. Our culture and habits might be slightly different, as are our names. Then, there is the food – delicious, tasty and spicy – that somehow seems to have been declared 'wrong'. But if what you eat decides what side you are on, then I should be on the 'wrong' side, too.

It was a sad lunch, because we understand that everything Zijo politely calls 'misunderstandings' – on both the Bosnian and the European sides – could perhaps have been avoided. Ever since that day in Stockholm, Europe has had another meaning for me. Every time I mention that word, I see the Bosnian family in front of me, living far away from whatever they call home and eating their own wonderful food because that's all that is left for them. The fact remains that, after fifty years, it was possible after all to have another war in Europe; that it was possible to change borders; that genocide is still possible even today. This should be enough to scare us all. This, and the fact that 'Europeans' – that is, people in France, Great Britain, Germany, Italy, Austria or Spain – watched all this, paralysed. It was all there, on the television screens in their living rooms, shells, bombs, slaughter, rape, blood, destruction – the entire war unfolded in front of their eyes. Everybody knew what was going on and this, in a way, is the curse of the war in Bosnia, in the Balkans, and in – well, in what is called Europe.

Should we not, must we not ask, then, what is Europe after Bosnia?